T'ai-chi's Ancestors:
The Making of an Internal Martial Art

Other titles distributed by Sweet Ch'i Press of interest to readers of this book:

Master Cheng's Thirteen Chapters on T'ai-chi Ch'uan
T'ai-chi Touchstones: Yang Family Secret Transmissions
Cheng Man-ch'ing's Advanced T'ai-chi Form Instructions with Selected Writings on Meditation, Medicine, the I ching, and the Arts
The Healing Herbs of China (wall chart)
Art of the Bed Chamber: The Chinese Sexual Yoga Classics, Including Women's Solo Meditation Texts
Lost T'ai-chi Classics from the Late Ch'ing Dynasty

T'ai-chi's Ancestors

The Making of an
Internal Martial Art

Douglas Wile

Sweet Ch'i Press

Published by Sweet Ch'i Press

Printed in the Unitied States of America

For information, address Sweet Ch'i Press
689 South Mountain Road, New City, NY 10956

Book design and typesetting by David Goodrich
Typefaces include Agfa Wile for body text,
Bitstream Calligraphic 421 for display,
and Union Way Fang Song for Chinese

Cover design by John Salerno
ISBN: 978-0-912059-04-4

10 9 8 7 6 5 4 3

This book is dedicated to
my parents, sister, wife and children

Contents

Note on Transliteration

The Wade-Giles system of transliteration has been adopted for this book as it is still the standard for library cataloguing. Mass media conversion to the Hanyu pinyin system in recent years, however, has made many words, particulary place and personal names, more familiar to readers in pinyin romanization. Therefore, with the exception of common place names, chiefly major cities and provinces, all other transliterations follow the modified Wade-Giles system.

1

General Introduction

T'ai-chi ch'üan cannot be captured by definitions, stick figures, or the camera; like religion or art, it is a complex creature of construction and interpretation. Its multiple personalities are the sum of its sources—physical and intellectual. T'ai-chi has a relatively stable nucleus of movement principles and internal energetics, but a cell membrane that interacts with great fluidity to its environment. As nurture often supercedes nature, the narrative in which the body mechanics are wrapped may be more important in conditioning the actual experience and influence of the art than the body mechanics themselves. This book introduces three sixteenth to eighteenth century traditions that contributed critical genetic material to the construction of t'ai-chi ch'üan in the late imperial–early Republican period. These three traditions have virtually vanished, but either their form, spirit, or theory live on in t'ai-chi ch'üan today. This book looks at the contribution of three men—a general, a peasant, and a scholar—to the making of t'ai-chi ch'üan. Ch'i Chi-kuang's *Essentials of the Classic of Pugilism* bequeathed its postures and form, Wang Cheng-nan's *Art of the Internal School* contributed its philosophy and ideology, and Ch'ang Nai-chou's writings share much of the language and theory of the t'ai-chi classics. Taken together these three truly are t'ai-chi's ancestors.

If t'ai-chi's genesis cannot be viewed as a single act of revelation or as an a priori set of perennial principles, this places it squarely in the realm of history and culture. As such, it is susceptible to deconstruction and tracing of influences, but we must go beyond clichés that simply take t'ai-chi as a synthesis of martial arts, military strategy, meditation, medicine, philosophy, and the like. To analyze it merely as an assembly of off-the-shelf cultural components does not tell us what role it has played in Chinese culture over time, how it enters the Western bloodstream, and how it is lived by practitioners. We are looking for motivation and meaning. It's role in China's collective national project is essential to understanding its history, but "strengthening the race and saving the nation" or "promoting health and serving the people" are not narratives that ressonate in the West, where individual self-empowerment or orientalist phansasies are more likely to animate practitioners. In terms of its form, all styles can be traced to the Ch'en family forms, and the Ch'en form in turn is derived from Ch'i Chi-kuang's sixteenth century *Classic of Pugilism*. Without Single Whip, Golden Cock Stands on One Leg, Patting the Horse, and so forth, t'ai-chi would be unrecognizable. The *Art of the Internal School*, described by Wang Cheng-nan and recorded by Huang Tsung-hsi and son Huang Pai-chia in the seventeenth century, gave t'ai-chi ch'üan its identity, its mission, its mythos, and its place in the culture. Ch'i's form is synthetic and pragmatic, a distillation of sixteen styles, whereas the Internal School projects itself as pure, transcendent, and unique. Ch'ang Nai-chou's eighteenth century theoretical writings and his Twenty-Four Character Form represent t'ai-chi's nurture, its education, and its substance. Although the links between Ch'ang and the putative Wang Tsung-yüeh, Ch'en Village, or the works written or redacted by Wu Yü-hsiang and Li Yi-yü have yet to be established, nevertheless, they speak the same language and are either parent and child or children of the same mother.

T'ai-chi's fate has been very much bound up with the fate of the nation. It emerged into public light in the nineteen century under elite and even Manchu patronage during a time of striving for national identity and self-strengthening. It was promoted in the twentieth century by both Nationalists and Communists as a treasure of traditional culture that could be salvaged from the feudal past and popularized for the nation's health. How does t'ai-chi fit into Chinese martial arts; how do martial arts fit into physical culture; and how does physical culture fit into general culture? With its origins in hunting, war dances, and military training, martial arts go back to the stone age. From at least the classical period forward, the Chinese ideal of civilian rule by a sage emperor and scholar-officials is in sharp contrast to the Western ideal of warrior rulers. New Chinese dynasties were usually swept into power on the crest of military might, but peasant soldiers were quickly disarmed and resettled on the land. In an agrarian society, warfare was extremely disruptive, and wealth was typically accumulated not by conquest but by squeezing surplus from the peasantry. Peasant productivity was a jealously guarded prize by Chinese landlords, who relied on the same population they were exploiting to rally to their defense when "barbarians" swarmed over the Great Wall or bombarded the seaports. Peasants trained in military arts returned home from battlefields with dangerous skills. These were often passed down to children and clansmen and could be turned on landlords, magistrates, and the ruling dynasty, given the right mix of natural disasters, hoarding, corruption, taxes, corvée, and landlessness.

Allusions to soft-style martial arts theory go back to the classical period. Chinese history and literature record two interesting encounters between martial artists and monarchs. The *Wu-Yüeh ch'un-ch'iu* (Annals of the states of Wu and Yüeh) compiled during the Han (206BCE–221CE) relates a dialogue between the King of Yüeh and a woman warrior named Yüeh Nü. In response to the King's plea for advice on how to strengthen his military, she reveals the secrets of her skill:

The art of swordsmanship is extremely subtle and elusive; its principles are most secret and profound. The tao has its gate and door, its yin and yang. Open the gate and close the door; yin declines and yang rises. When practicing the art of hand-to-hand combat, concentrate your spirit internally and give the impression of relaxation externally. You should look like a

MAJOR
DON'T LET THEM SEE YOU COMING.

modest woman and strike like a ferocious tiger. As you assume various postures, regulate your ch'i, moving always with the spirit. Your skill should be as obvious as the sun and as startling as a bolting hare. Your opponent endeavors to pursue your form and chase your shadow, yet your image hovers between existence and non-existence. The breath moves in and out and should never be held. Whether you close with the opponent vertically or horizontally, with or against the flow, never attack frontally. Mastery of this art allows one to match a hundred, and a hundred to match a thousand. If your Highness would like to test it, I can demonstrate for your edification.[1]

Here we find the principles, and even some of the poetic language, of the t'ai-chi classics as we know them two thousand years later. The dialogue between ruler and specialist was typical of the time, but later gave way to the essay or treatise style. This very short passage contains all the elements of strategy, internal energetics, psychology, and yin-yang theory we associate with later t'ai-chi writings.

*   *   *

The seminal Taoist classic the *Chuang tzu* includes a chapter entitled "On swordsmanship" (Shuo chien 説劍), that is a philosophical parable, a lesson in swordsmanship, and also an exposé of the dark side of the martial arts. Chuang tzu's story tells of King Wen of the state of Chao, who was such a fanatic patron of fencing that three thousand gladiators flocked to his court. Vying to satisfy the King's sadistic taste, more than a hundred swordsman died each year. The nation was suffering from neglect, and the feudal lords were plotting his overthrow. Prince K'uei appealed to Chuang tzu to pursuade the King to desist from his perverse pleasures, and Chuang tzu agreed to take the case. Presenting himself to the King as an invincible swordsman, he began by expounding his philosophy of swordsmanship: "The art of swordsmanship is to give the opponent the impression of an opening and offer him an opportunity to attack. I move only after he does, but my sword lands first."[2] The King was impressed with this exposition and was anxious to test Chuang tzu against the best in his stable. Chuang tzu requested that he first be allowed to tell the King a story, and by the end of his parable he had made the King realize that, while occupying the most exhaulted position in the land, he had stooped to the level of cock fighting with human beings. In both Yüeh Nü and Chuang tzu we have intimations of not only soft-style strategy, but internal ch'i cultivation as well.

Having long been judged irrelevant to mass warfare, that is, useless to the state, martial arts were forced to cling to the margins of society in the form of bodyguard brotherhoods, secret societies, operatic performances, fairgrounds' exhibitions, banditry, and knight-errantry. Knight-errantry flourished in folklore, but in fact was indistinguishable from banditry in the eyes of the state. For Ming general Ch'i Chi-kuang, the priority was mass warfare: he could exercise righteous violence on behalf of the Ming state against northern barbarians and Japanese pirates; for Huang Tsung-hsi, knight-errantry was the only alternative, and he took personal initiative first against the corrupt Ming court and later the occupying Manchu regime. Here we see a clear shift in narrative. During the Mongol dynasty (1271–1368), the Han Chinese were forbidden to own weapons or engage in hunting; they were subject to curfew and restricted in the areas of assembly, religious sects, and martial arts.[3] During the Manchu dynasty, once again the state attempted to enforce a monopoly of martial skills, and an edict of 1727 proclaims:

There are individuals who practice the martial arts, and calling themselves masters, seduce the masses and stir up ignorant people. . . . Belligerent young men flock to them, abandoning productive occupations and spending all day building themselves up and sparring with each other. . . . Sometimes they assume the name of religion to assemble thieves and bandits and harass the local population. Some claim that the practice of martial arts among the people allows them to defend themselves and avoid humiliation, but are they unaware that if people are law-abiding, well-behaved, and humble, then banditry would disappear and conflicts vanish? What need is there of martial arts for self-defense? It is the responsibility of all officials to ban them. Teachers and students will be strictly prosecuted.[4]

Whether practiced to defend the state against external invasion or to oppose an alien regime, martial arts have always functioned in a political context, and even stylistic differences have often reflected political ideologies.

2

Ch'i Chi-kuang's
«Essentials of the Classic of Pugilism»

Introduction

The Mongol dynasty, although short-lived by Chinese standards, nevertheless lasted three generations, long enough for a man to be born and die of old age within its span. Of the three arenas in which martial arts were normally practiced—military, theatrical, and private—the military and private were banned to Han Chinese during this period of foreign rule, and as a result, theatrical martial arts reached unprecedented heights. The civil service examinations being abolished, theatre also became one of the only outlets for literary talent. Literature and martial arts, traditional rivals, now found themselves in the same boat, or should we say, on the same stage. This was also a period of demoralization for the martial spirit in China, as the preeminent empire of the East now found herself not only ruled by Mongol aliens, but the jewel in the crown of their universal empire stretching from Korea to the Danube.

With the restoration of Chinese rule during the Ming (1368–1644), the three arenas of martial arts practice once again sprang back to life. Although artillery already played a significant role in military operations, the skill of infantry with swords and spears was still decisive. However, by the sixteenth century, the imperial army had become so weak and ineffective that it was powerless to repel bands of Japanese pirates, who not only controlled China's coastal waters, but plundered the provinces of the littoral with impunity, especially Jiangsu, Fujian, Zhejiang, and Guangdong. In the 1540s and 50s, the Tartars of the north breached the Great Wall and even sacked Beijing. In 1592 the Japanese laid siege to Korea and were not expelled by the Chinese until 1598. The sixteenth century also saw the beginnings of a whole new threat when Portugal seized Macao in 1535. The great Ming general Ch'i Chi-kuang's (1528–1587) patriotic response to these incursions was to have a far-reaching influence on the nation and indirectly on the development of t'ai-chi ch'üan.

Ch'i was born in 1528 to a distinguished Shantung military family. The Ch'i family had served for generations as commanders of the garrison in their native Tengchou County, and at seventeen Chi-kuang, too, joined the garrison. In 1548 he was assigned to a battalion protecting Jimen in the northeast corner of Beijing and first showed his mettle in defending the capital against Mongol incursions. In 1555 he was sent south to organize eradication of the Japanese pirate plague, and establishing his headquarters in Ningbo, recruited and trained a crack corps of Zhejiang braves. Rigorous and regular testing threatened those who failed with demotion to cooks, and killing first born sons was the punishment for any who looked back in battle. Following his successful campaign of pirate pacification, he was called north in 1568, when he brought his elite Zhejiang troops to form the nucleus of forces protecting the capital until 1583. After court slander and reassignment to Guangtong, he retired in 1885 to his hometown. Ch'i's use of the *Classic of Pugilism* to train troops in the north may explain how it found its way into Ch'en Village, where in 1931 and 1932 T'ang Hao found copies of Ch'i's writings and determined that the Ch'en family forms were based on the *Classic*.

Ch'i was no academic or armchair general: he believed that military science was an empirical and constantly evolving science and not one that could be mastered by merely perusing the classics. Motivated by a strong sense of shame for China's weakness, he led by example and strict discipline. To this end, he created a force in Zhejiang, one of the front line provinces, personally trained by him and subject to a discipline that set it strictly apart from the typical troops. Imperial impotence and the formation of a special mission army with a strong regional base was a strategy revisited during the Ch'ing, when the Hunan army of Tseng Kuo-fan helped put down the Taiping Rebellion. Ch'i belonged to a generation of patriots, who, caught between imperial ineptitude and foreign aggression, took personal initiative and lived out the Confucian narrative of saving the nation, only to be slandered by sycophants and die in bitter but creative seclusion. In this sense, his life very much parallels that of Huang Tsung-hsi, who brought the Internal School to light a hundred years later. Ch'i had many comrades in arms who rose from humble origins to become field commanders and military reformers and left behind records of their experience for future generations. These include T'ang Shun-chih, Yü Ta-yu, Ho Liang-ch'en, Cheng Jo-ts'eng, Wu Shu, and Mao Yüan-i. Of all these, Ch'i's work proved to be most influential, being reprinted over and over in China and reproduced under different titles in Japan and Korea. Bitter and frustrated following slander and virtual exile, he retired to his home to organize a lifetime of writing on every aspect of military science and published a series of works that were for subsequent generations second only to Sun tzu's *Art of War*. His works on military science include *Effective New Methods in Military Science* (Chi-hsiao hsin-shu 紀效新書), *Practical Troop Training* (Lien-ping shih-chi 練兵實紀), *New Military Manual* (Wu-pei hsin-shu 武備新書), *Outline of Military Science* (Li-jung yao-lüeh 蒞戎要略), and general works of poetry and prose, *Collected Works from the Chih-chih Hall* (Chih-chih t'ang chi 止止堂集) and *Heart Seal of an Elder Brother* (Chang-tzu hsin-ch'ien 長子心鈐).

General Ch'i's undying contribution to t'ai-chi ch'üan is that he personally studied sixteen different martial arts and synthesized them into a thirty-two posture form intended for troop training. He made similar efforts in the realm of weapons, receiving pointers on spear from T'ang Shun-chih (1507–1560) and on staff from Yü Ta-yu (1504–1580). His training regimen included lifting sandbags to increase body strength, training with weighted weapons to develop arm strength, and running with ankle weights to strengthen legs and build stamina. Ch'i's form provided a standard set that transcended family lineages and could be widely adopted and absorbed. Ch'i's creation of a synthetic and standardized form in the sixteenth century gives us a glimpse of the variety of styles current at that time and prefigures state sponsored simplified and competition forms promoted in the People's Republic of China since 1949. Calling his new creation a "classic" is an unusual touch, but garnishing it with verse instructions was probably not a shock to contemporaries and has been a familiar feature of martial arts literature down to modern times.

Pioneer martial arts researcher T'ang Hao paid Ch'i's *Classic of Pugilism* the highest praise when he said: "Ch'i's *Classic of Pugilism* must be considered the oldest martial arts manual since the six works listed in the *History of the Han Dynasty* bibliography."[1] This leaves a 1700 year gap in the record, and Ch'i's work is all the more precious since none of the Han works are extant. Ch'i's contemporary and fellow military scientist Mao Yüan-yi explained the cultural background of this anomaly when he said: "Ch'en Ssu-wang was a great man of letters, but when it came to martial arts, he could also wax eloquent. Why is it that people today are embarrased to speak of pugilism?"[2]

Ch'i claims to have collected and surveyed both ancient and contemporary styles, but because of grammatical ambiguities in the original, commentators have disagreed over which in the list of sixteen styles Ch'i meant to represent the ancient and which the contemporary, and even how different punctuation would yield different lists. There are also some discrepancies between the *Ch'üan ching* catalogue and those in T'ang Shun-chih's *Wu pien*, Wu Shu's *Shou-pi lu,* and Ho Liang-ch'en's *Chen chi.* Some scholars have attempted to make something of the coincidence that Zhejiang, where Ch'i based his recruiting, was also the home of the Internal School, immortalized by Huang Tsung-hsi. They even try to equate the "Wen Family Boxing" listed by Ch'i with the Wenchou mentioned in Huang's "Epitaph" as the home of Ch'en Chou-t'ung, who learned from Wang

Tsung. According to Huang's geneology, after many transmissions it was passed to Chang Sung-hsi, who is recorded in the *Ningbo Gazetteer*, and finally in an unbroken line to Wang Cheng-nan, the subject of Huang's "Epitaph" and the informant for the younger Huang's *Art of the Internal School*. Unfortunately, Ch'i himself makes no mention of the Internal School in Wenchou or any special martial tradition or aptitude there. Even Ho Liang-ch'en, who shared Ch'i's keen interest in surveying and recording local martial arts, and who was himself a native of Huang Pai-chia's Yü-yao County in Zhejiang, made no mention of any remarkable martial art in this area, let alone one as unique as the Internal School.

T'ang Shun-chih's *Wu pien* is highly derivative of Ch'i's work, but contains a number of unique details that shed additional light on the *Classic of Pugilism*. T'ang records several passages from the manuals of the Wen Family art, which when placed alongside the *Classic of Pugilism's* thirty-two postures reveal five that are identical or closely parallel in name. As Ch'i himself explains, he followed the principle of selecting the best features of each of the sixteen styles in order to create a balanced art. In his 1937 "Ch'i Chi-kuang's *Classic of Pugilism*"[3] T'ang Hao listed 25 postures from the *Classic of Pugilism*[4] that can be found in the Ch'en Family forms, along with language paralleling that in the *Classic*. However, Ku Liu-hsin points out in his *T'ai-chi ch'üan shu* that the earliest extant edition of Ch'i's *Chi-hsiao hsin-shu* dates from 1595 and is missing text and illustrations for numbers 15, 16, 17, 18, 21, 22, 23, and 24. Among these eight additional postures, four correspond to those in Ch'en family forms, and thus the total of postures taken from the *Classic of Pugilism* "comes to twenty-nine." This combined with T'ang Hao's discovery of copies of Ch'i's works among the Ch'en family manuscripts reinforces the influence of Ch'i on the development of t'ai-chi ch'üan. Subsequent editions, including those examined by T'ang Hao, were also marred by the same omisssion. The *Ku-chin t'u-shu chi-ch'eng* encyclopedia, compiled in the early Ch'ing (17th cent.), contains no illustrations, but does include all thirty-two texts. Finally in 1956, Ku Liu-hsin discovered a complete version of both text and illustrations in Mao Yüan-yi's *Wu-pei chih* (1621).[5] Li Sung-fu discovered that the *San-ts'ai t'u-hui* of the Ming Wan-li period (1573–1620) contained all thirty-two texts and illustrations, but in slightly confused order, and even more surprisingly, without the author's name. The latter is especially strange since Wang Ch'i, the author of the *San-tsai t'u-hui*, and Ch'i Chi-kuang were contemporaries.

Ch'i's motivation for creating the thirty-two posture *Classic* was, of course, to create a standard training form for troops. His broad background and survey of ancient and current styles allowed him to select the superior points of every style, avoid their deficiencies, and create a synthesis that would be "complete both above and below." Another motivation was to purge the martial arts of "flowery postures" and return the art to its practical foundations at a time when China was harassed by Japan, Portugal, and the northern "barbarians." In Chap. 4 of his *Lien-ping shih-chi*, Ch'i expresses his opposition to "flowery forms": "In practicing the martial arts, you should imagine that you are striking an actual opponent and not just study superficial techniques."[6] One of the characteristics of "flowery forms" was a misunderstanding of the function of postures. In his introduction to the *Classic of Pugilism* Ch'i admonishes his readers: "Without obvious postures or techniques, you will be effective with one move; if you do make the mistake of posturing and posing, you will be ineffective with ten moves." T'ang Shun-chih's *Wu pien* reproduces and expands upon much of the material in Ch'i's work, and speaks specifically to this question of postures in a way that serves as a footnote to Ch'i's remarks: "The reason for postures in the martial arts is to facilitate transformations.... Forms contain fixed postures, but in actual practice there are no fixed postures. When applied they become fluid, but still maintain their structural characteristics." T'ang also explains the questions of full and empty, and long and short range techniques. He considers the feint to be "empty" and the true attack "full" and insists that full and empty, long and short, must all be balanced in order to qualify as a complete art. Finally: "Once you have learned the form, you must engage in sparring."[7] More than a thousand years earlier the great Taoist Ko Hung (283–363) pointed to just this problem when describing military training in his youth: "We trained without an opponent and had no practical experience."[8] Exhibition forms have always been a part of Chinese fairs, banquets, and market places, and even a subject for equally flowery literary productions. Ch'i's fellow anti-Japanese general T'ang Shun-chih in his "Song of the Omei Taoist's Martial Art" gives us a flavor of this kind of martial arts dance:

Suddenly a vertical kick shoots straight up,
Smashing cliffs and scattering sand.
Back and forth, the celestial Weaving Maid throws the
    divine shuttle,
As devils and demons flap their green sleeves.
Wheeling around and pointing with his finger, the chariot
    of the sun stops in its track.
Withdrawing his head and drilling diagonally, he pierces
    with needle eyes.
With a hundred bends of the waist, he seems utterly bone-
    less,
And giving free expression to his energy, hands grew from
    his entire body."[9]

If the *Classic of Pugilism* gave its outer form to what would later become t'ai-chi ch'üan, is it also possible to find the seeds of t'ai-chi's soft-style principles in Ch'i's writings or those of his contemporaries as well? Among the styles that Ch'i surveyed was one called "Cotton Chang's Close Boxing." Ch'i places this art in a context that implies a hard-soft analysis of styles, and he seems to express a preference for the latter: "Lu Hung's Eight Throws, although it is hard, is not as good as Cotton Chang's Close Boxing." In describing the movement qualities recommended for practicing his form, he says, "its softness expresses itself in dodging and evading," and "each posture follows the previous in order," indicating an appreciation of the roles of softness and continuity. Fellow anti-Japanese general Yü

Ta-yu (1503–1580) was famous for his skill in staff and wrote the *Classic of Swordsmanship*, actually a treatise on staff, which he considered the mother of all weapons. This work was published in Yü's *Cheng-ch'i t'ang chi* and also reproduced in Ch'i's *Chi-hsiao hsin-shu*. It is in this work that I find the first appearance of the word "sticking" (*nien*) in martial arts literature. Wu Yü-hsiang's nineteenth century t'ai-chi classic, the "Ta-shou yao-yen," contains the phrase: "If the opponent does not move, I do not move; if the opponent makes the slightest move, I strike first." This principle can be traced back to the sixteenth century, when Yü wrote, "Just before issuing energy, the opponent is hard. I take advantage of the softness that follows his issuing energy. The opponent is flustered, while I wait in stillness, playing with him as he struggles."[10] In between these two is Huang Tsung-hsi's seventeenth century characterization of the relative merits of hard and soft styles: "Shao-lin is famous for its boxers. However, its techniques are chiefly offensive, which creates opportunities for an opponent to exploit." Long before any of these, however, was the *Sun tzu ping-fa* (Sun tzu's art of war), which says: "I allow the enemy to initiate the attack, but my blow lands first" and "I wait in calmness for the enemy's weariness."[11] Familiar martial arts metaphors such as "water" and theortical tools like "full and empty" can also be traced back to the venerable Sun tzu: "The highest military formation is formless....Military formations should be like water. Water avoids the high places and seeks the low. Military formations avoid the enemy's fullness and attack his emptiness."[12] Sun tzu was also aware of the collective ch'i, or morale, of an army when he says: "The morning ch'i is sharp; the afternoon ch'i is lazy; and the evening ch'i retiring. Therefore, the superior strategist avoids the enemy's sharp ch'i and attacks his lazy and retiring ch'i."[13] These phrases were very much a part of the thinking of sixteenth century military theorists like Ch'i and his colleagues, and also find their way into the t'ai-chi literature in the eighteenth and nineteenth centuries.

Ho Liang-ch'en's *Chen chi* develops a number of Sun tzu's ideas which later became an integral part of t'ai-chi tactics. He speaks of surprise, ch'i, and spontaneity. Contrasting surprise and conventional tactics, Ho defines surprise as more than just sneak attacks: "Our stillness is a surprise for an impatient enemy; our discipline is a surprise for a confused enemy; our sufficiency is a surprise for a hungry enemy; our ease is a surprise for a weary enemy.... anything can be a surprise."[14] T'ang Shun-chih in his *Wu pien* identifies surprise as "emptiness" and conventional assault as "fullness." This is a departure from Sun tzu, who used emptiness to represent weakness and fullness for strength. Sun tzu said colorfully: "The use of military force is like throwing a rock at an egg; this is what is meant by full and empty."[15] Deception was used, according to Sun tzu, to empty the enemy's fullness and sap his strength. In t'ai-chi literature, a weight-bearing leg or energy issuing hand are considered full. This shows the flexibility of the basic stock of scientific terminology derived from the *I ching*. On the question of ch'i, Ho believed that troops must be instilled with "life or death ch'i," which could come from fighting with their backs to water, executing deserters, or best of all, fighting for a just cause.[16] Sun tzu taught that deep penetration of enemy territory caused one's own troops to become concentrated and courageous. The *Wei Liao tzu*, one of the seven ancient military classics, has a slightly different twist on military psychology. It says: "When fighting for a righteous cause, strike first; when fighting for spoils, let the enemy strike first."[17] In the *Wei Liao tzu's*: "An army gains victory through stillness"[18] and the *San lüeh's*: "Softness can control hardness; weakness can control strength,"[19] we can see that traditional Chinese military strategy is a rich source for t'ai-chi tactics and philosophy.

On the question of spontaneity, Ho's words resonate so strikingly with the t'ai-chi literature that it is clear they share the same cultural matrix. In describing the harmony between officers and troops, he uses the individual as microcosm and the army as macrocosm:

"The mind directs the body, the body mobilizes the arms, and the arms use the fingers. Movement and stillness are sponta-

neous under the direction of the mind....The able general
directs his forces as spontaneously as the scattering of winds,
the gathering of clouds, or a great rock rolling down a high
mountain and crashing into a pool of water. The enemy cannot foresee his attack or resist him."[20]

Ho expresses the concept of mental calmness when he writes of
archery: "The principle of archery is to pull the bow powerfully and
to full measure and to release the arrow calmly and with a spacious
mind."[21] We are accustomed to thinking of t'ai-chi ch'üan as a mul-
tifaceted art, practiced for health, meditation, and self-defense, and
showing the confluence of martial arts, meditation, philosophy, military strategy, and medicine. However, military science was itself an
eclectic discipline, requiring expertise in engineering, geography, logistics, psychology, and martial arts. Even meditation and occultism
were absorbed into military science, as we see in T'ang Shun-chih's
Wu pien, which contains detailed directions for the general to practice microcosmic orbit meditation (*hsiao chou-t'ien*) while writing charms
(*fu*) to obtain victory.[22]

One senses a certain ambivalence in Ch'i Chi-kuang's attitude
toward the martial arts. What role did he feel they played in society?
The *Classic of Pugilism* was included in the *Chi-hsiao hsin-shu* with the
disclaimer: "The techniques of bare-handed combat would seem to
have little relevance to the science of mass warfare." It is clear from
the pains he took to survey, and probably to learn, so many different
styles that martial arts was undoubtedly a lifelong avocation, but as
a good Confucian his primary interest was defense of the nation, and
thus he considered logistics, formations, tactics, and the like to be
the decisive factors. As early as Hsün tzu (fl. 298–238 BC), there
was a skeptical strain in Chinese thought regarding the value of
individual martial virtuosity. Hsün tzu said in his "I ping" (On military science): "The people of the state of Ch'i value martial arts and
reward their soldiers according to the number of enemy they kill.
While this may enable you to overcome a weak enemy, it will not

work against a strong one."[23] Skepticism regarding the effectiveness of martial arts masters in the ranks is seen in the reflections of Ch'i's contemporary Hsieh Chao-che, whose *Wu tsa tzu* states: " Bare-handed combat is one of the 'eighteen martial skills.' There is a man called Hsiao Ssu-p'u, who is an invincible martial artist and is like a little tiger. There is another man called Liang Hsing-fu, who is a martial arts hero in his village, but these types are useless on the battlefield."[24] The literati rejected the martial arts as brutish and unrefined, and statesmen castigated them as a menace to domestic tranquility, but it is perhaps less well known that even generals had their reservations. In his *Chiang-nan ching-lüeh*, Ch'i's contemporary Cheng Jo-tseng advises: "Martial skills can be acquired after recruitment and should not be a basis for selection."[25] "Ch'i advocates the use of his thirty-two posture form as much for confidence building as for conditioning and skills acquisition: "Mastery of his art makes a man brave." Or, as Ho Liang-ch'en put it: "To develop courage and spirit, train them in the martial arts."[26] Thus popular arts developed among the masses were appropriated, synthesized, and used for state sponsored ends. State sponsorship then became the unwitting vehicle for wider desemination of the art among the people. Ch'i certainly acknowledges the popular roots of his *Classic*, but we do not find him promoting it as a regimen for civilian consumption, unlike during the twentieth century, when martial arts were called upon to rebuild the health of the "race" and restore the martial spirit to the national ethos.

Essentials of the Classic of Pugilism[1]

by CH'I CHI-KUANG

The techniques of bare-handed combat would seem to have little relevance to the science of mass warfare. However, from the point of view of exercising the limbs and training the body, this is the best introduction. For this reason, we include it at the end of this work to complete the requirements for mastery of the art of war.

The study of pugilism requires agility of the body, dexterity of the hands, and lightness and stability of the feet. When advancing and withdrawing are properly adjusted, the legs will seem to fly. The subtlety of this art is seen in rising, falling, turning, and thrusting; its fierceness in splitting with a horizontal chop; its speed in seizing and throwing the opponent flat on his back; and its softness in knowing when to dodge and evade. Therefore, I have chosen the thirty-two best postures, each posture following the previous in order. When your art is invincible, infinite, and unfathomable; when it is obscure and mysterious; when none can spy its secrets, then at this level, it may be called miraculous.

There is a saying, "Not knowing the art of pugilism is like thunder striking with no time to cover the ears." This is what is meant by, "When you go beyond postures and techniques, you will be effective with one move; if you do make the mistake of posturing and posing, you will be ineffective with ten moves." Victory belongs to those who study widely and plan carefully.

Among martial arts styles past and present, there are "Emperor T'ai-tsu of the Sung's Thirty-two Posture Long Boxing," and also "Six Step Boxing," "Monkey Boxing," and "Decoy Boxing." Although the names and postures differ somewhat, in reality, the distinctions are minimal. Among the best of contemporary styles are the "Wen Family Seventy-two Posture Moving Form," "Thirty-six Posture Locking Form," "Twenty-four Throws Pat on Horse,"[2] "Eight Evasive Maneuvers" and "Twelve Postures Close Boxing." "Lu Hung's Eight Throws," although it is hard, is not as good as "Cotton Chang's Close Boxing." Li Pan-t'ien of Shantung's leg techniques, Eagle Claw Wang's grappling techniques, Thousand Falls Chang's falling techniques, Chang Po-ching's striking techniques, the Shao-lin Temple's staff techniques and those of Ch'ing-t'ien, Yang Family spear techniques, and Pa tzu's boxing and staff are all famous today. Although each of these is superior in some respects, they are all guilty of either emphasizing the top to the neglect of the bottom, or the bottom to the neglect of the top. Even if one is successful in overcoming an opponent with these styles, this is no more than one-sided mastery. However, if one were to practice all of these styles in combination, this would be like the battlefield deployment known as "Mount Ch'ang Snake Formation." If the head is attacked, the tail counter-attacks; if the tail is attacked, the head counter-attacks; and if the body is attacked, the head and tail both counter-attack. This is what we mean by mastery of both above and below, and victory is assured.

In general, the hand, staff, broadsword, spear, fork, claw, two-edged sword, two-pronged spear, bow and arrow, hooked sword, sickle, and shield all proceed from bare-handed techniques to train the body and hands. Bare-handed techniques are the foundation of the martial arts.

Herein we have illustrated the postures and annotated them with aphorisms to enlighten future students. Having acquired the art, it should be tested against an opponent. Victory or defeat should not be the cause of wonder, but the occasion for pondering the reason for victory or defeat. If you examine the situation for a long time, you will discover that a cowardly opponent is one who lacks skill, while a successful warrior is one who has mastered his art. There is an ancient saying that goes, "Mastery of his art makes a man brave." Surely there is much truth in this.

I

"Leisurely Tucking in the Garments" is a posture for coming out to
    face the opponent
That can transform into lower style "Quick Step" or "Single Whip."
If the opponent lacks the courage to advance,
I stand impassively with clear eyes and relaxed hands.

2

"Golden Cock Stands on One Leg" lowers and raises.
Feint with the leg and strike sideways with the fist.
Throw the opponent on his back with arms and legs in the air.
When the opponent encounters this technique, his cries will reach
    high heaven.

3

"Patting the Horse" was transmitted by Emperor T'ai-tsu of the Sung.
Every posture can be lowered or transformed.
Attacking or evading, even the weak become strong.
This posture is superior for receiving a close attack.

4

"Bend Single Whip" as chrysanthemum presses closely.
Deflect the opponent's challenging legs to the left and right so that
    he can barely defend himself.
Advance boldly, raise your fist, and split and expose.
"Profound Fragrance Posture" can topple Mount T'ai.

5

In "Seven Stars Posture," hands and feet face each other.
Close with the opponent, pressing above and raising the trap from
    below.
Even if his hands are fast and feet like the wind,
I can still undo him with my thrust and split.

6

"Riding the Dragon Backward" feigns defeat and pretends to run.
When the opponent has been lured into hot pursuit, I turn on him.
Let him attack with fierceness and force;
How can he withstand my relentless pounding?

7

"Suspending One Leg in Mid-Air" lures the opponent to casually
    approach,
But my two leg changes do not permit such casualness.
When I raise one hand, he will see a heaven full of stars.
Who would dare challenge me again?

8

"Ch'iu and Liu Posture" deflects left and strikes right.
When his chop comes and his steps bring him to my very heart,
I change my method to "Patting the Horse."
With a single blow the opponent's life is lost.

9

"Downward Thrust Posture" is designed to discourage fast legs.
It matters not whether the opponent charges, harasses, or leans,
For I hook his leg, lock his arm, and never let go.
Threatening above and seizing below, I throw him for a fall.

10

"Ambush Posture" is like bending the bow and waiting for a tiger.
If the opponent advances one inch into my trap, it will be hard for
    him to escape.
While I seize the moment to deliver repeated kicks,
The beaten opponent will be stunned and terrified.

II

"Throwing Posture" charges with a menacing chop,
That supplements the forward leg in plain sight.
Sweep to the right and seize to the left, as fast as flight.
Striking with the palm, your opponent will be rendered oblivious
   to heaven and earth.

12

"Fingering the Elbow Posture" prevents him from using his legs.
I block a close attack, always aware of high and low.
Whether chopping, striking, pushing, or pressing, I follow the
   opponent,
Never hasty with hands and feet.

13

"One Quick Step" seizes opportunities and responds to changes.
I repeatedly strike the opponent to the left and right.
No matter that his stances are powerful and his hands like storms;
How could he withstand my evasion, feints, and subtle seizing.

14

"Grappling Posture" is used for trapping the opponent's feet.
Press him left and right just like "Four Levels."
Although he attacks me head on, I am unaffected,
And even his fast feet will meet with no success.

15

"Well Railing Four Levels" advances straight ahead.
When the opponent attempts to scissor my lower leg and kick my knee,
I roll and insert a chop and a shoulder, swiping with a hook,
So that even a hero of iron would turn and flee.

16

"Ghost Kick" steals the opponent's first thunder.
Guard your front, sweep and turn, and put out a red fist.
Shoulder the bow, split with the head, and disarm the opponent rising.
Penetrating his defenses with elbow or shoulder is difficult to master.

17

"Aim for the Crotch" is a technique designed for males.
It is difficult for him to advance, but I easily push forward.
With a kick to the knee, I roll and thrust upward,
Quickly withdrawing and delivering a red fist at close range.

18

"Animal Head Posture" advances with an erect stance.
Let the opponent's fast feet confront me with confusion and haste,
While I feint high and strike low, putting the opponent in great
    jeopardy.
Catching his close strike, I thrust upward with a red fist.

19

"Middle Four Levels Posture" topples the opponent's solid stance.
His hard attack and fast legs will find it difficult to approach me,
As I use two hands to press his single hand.
In close combat, training is the key.

20

"Crouching Tiger Posture" turns to the side and levels a kick.
If the opponent approaches me, poling forward like a boat,
I notice his lack of stability,
And sweep him from behind so that he falls.

21

"High Four Levels" posture excels at rapid changes.
If the opponent weaves swiftly left and right, in and out,
I press him so that his hands and feet are useless,
While I freely kick and punch.

22

"Backward Thrust Posture" offers no stance or posture.
When the opponent tries to gain an easy victory with quick legs,
I arch the back and advance without delay,
And strike like thunder echoing in a valley.

23

"Spirit Fist" thrusts downward, directly facing the opponent.
If he advances with a flame that builds up at my chest,
He will meet with my skillful seizing and throws.
When you raise your hand, show no mercy to your opponent.

24

"One Lash" splits and chops with a horizontal and a vertical.
If the opponent advances with both feet, attempting to inflict
    damage head on,
I care not that his strength is great and his blood is hot,
For my superior skill will win the day.

25

"Dragon Alights On Ground" is a technique for folding the legs.
I open his defense in front, rise up in back, and move in with a
    red fist.
While he retreats, I follow up
With a charge that gets in close and stops him cold.

26

"Hand Faces Heaven" turns the body to guard against a kick,
Then seamlessly forces the opponent into retreat.
Reversing my posture, I deliver a kick
That would level the greatest master.

27

"Wild Goose Wings" closes with the opponent, turning the body
  sideways.
As he moves quickly to escape,
I pursue him, inserting a kick,
Followed by a scissors, split, push, or punch.

28

"Tiger Riding Posture" moves into position to deliver a kick.
If he tries to escape, without letting him know,
I sweep him from the left and right repeatedly,
And when he is helpless, the scissors will divide him easily.

29

"Bend Phoenix Elbow" steps forward and chops,
Blocking down, seizing with the hand, and pounding the
    opponent's chest.
Grab his private parts, catch the rabbit, and draw the bow.
Hands and feet must be perfectly coordinated.

30

"Cannon Aimed at the Head" posture attacks with a fearful force.
The charging tiger seizes with both paws.
When he retreats to evade my attack, I once again kick him.
Even if he is not knocked down, he will still be in serious trouble.

31

"Tame Phoenix Elbow" leads with the shoulder and blocks.
I roll quickly so that the opponent has nowhere to hide.
Then again twisting and stroking from the outside, I tie him up.
With a blow to the belly he falls, not daring to close with me
      again.

32

"Banners and Drums Posture" presses forward left and right.
At close range, I use split in two directions.
Twisting and leaning into the opponent, he is thrown and realizes
That it is too late for even the tiger to hide his head.

3

Documents on the Internal School

Introduction

The Manchu conquest of China, consolidated in 1644, was the great divide in Huang's Tsung-hsi's life. The first half of his life was marked by political intrigue, rebellion, conquest, and guerrilla struggle, and the second half by research, reflection, and writing. Born in 1610 in Yü-yao County, Zhejiang Province, at the age of fourteen he followed his father to the capital Beijing, where the elder Huang had been appointed as an imperial censor. During this period, the court was dominated by a clique of corrupt eunuchs, who persecuted righteous officials and oppressed the masses with intolerable taxes. Concerned gentry reacted by forming the Tung-lin Party to oppose these excesses, and the peasants, led by Li Tzu-ch'eng, mounted a rebellion that was finally quelled only by the Manchu conquest itself. Political struggle between these two factions culminated in 1625 in the assassination or execution of Tung-lin members, including Huang's father. Just two years later, with a new more enlightened emperor on the throne and some of the corrupt officials swept away, Huang petitioned the Emperor to punish his father's persecutors. While testifying against them in criminal trial, the nineteen year old Tsung-hsi shocked the court and the whole nation by drawing a hidden awl from his sleeve and personally avenging his father's death by stabbing one of the principals. After spending a year in prison, he managed to escape in the chaos resulting from Manchu incursions.

Wu San-kuei's ill-conceived strategey of using the Manchus to put down the peasant rebellion backfired when the Manchus realized they were in a position to seize the whole prize for themselves. With north China occupied, the Manchus moved to mop up resistance in the South. After the fall of Nanjing and Hangzhou, Huang Tsung-hsi remained one of the last loyalists in Ningbo, and he continued to carry out guerrilla struggle for nearly ten years. He was a hunted man, his family members were persecuted, and, when in 1653 he could no longer rally resistance forces, he retired from public life, refusing to serve the alien dynasty in any capacity. The second half of his life was devoted to teaching and writing.

When Huang Tsung-hsi put down his sword and took up the pen, he undertook no less than a comprehensive critique of the whole intellectual tradition and political system that had led to the fall of the Ming dynasty. Unlike most Chinese thinkers and historians, he chose to focus not on ancient history, but on the period closest to his own times, the Sung, Yüan, and Ming dynasties. He was also unusual in condemning not just the lack of moral character in emperors and officials, but the autocratic institutions that made the people servants of the rulers rather than the rulers servants of the people.[1] Risking the label "Legalist"—Confucianism's age-old philosophical foe—Huang advocated a larger role for law in society and as a check against the arbitrary exercise of power. When it came to Taoism and Buddhism, however, he showed his Confucian social conscience by opposing these schools for promoting passivity and escapism. He has earned the title of "proto-materialist" by modern Marxist intellectual historians for declaring: "Between heaven and earth there is nothing but the movement of one ch'i,"[2] and for condemning the Sung School of the Mind's retreating to an inner psychological reality and the School of Reason's positing a transcendent realm of principle outside of the material world.

Much has been made of Huang Tsung-hsi and his son Pai-chia's use of martial arts master Wang Cheng-nan as a symbol for expressing their anti-Manchu politics. Historians have pointed out Wang's vow of vegetarianism until China's liberation and the Huangs' refusal to name the Ch'ing (Manchu) dynasty in expressing Wang's dates. In my *Lost T'ai-chi Classics from the Late Ch'ing Dynasty*, I suggest a political allegory in the "Epitaph's" assertion of the superiority of the Internal School over Shaolin as a coded strategy for China (internal) to overcome Manchu (external) rule. A deeper look at Huang's philosophy, however, reveals still another level of symbolism in the narrative of the "Epitaph." As an unlettered man and a patriot, Wang represents the need for an alliance between loyal literati and the masses. His martial prowess and patriotism were in part due to his having escaped the corrupting influence of a civil service education. Huang decried the effete tendencies in the ruling class, saying: "With the introduction of the civil service examination system, scholars sought to earn their keep by cultivating superficial elegance with no relevance to affairs of state."[3] Huang considered himself a Confucian and insisted that martial studies belonged in the Confucian curriculum: "When the north fell to the Manchus, armchair observers all said that a military response could not save the day. I alone disagreed. In ancient times military arts were an integral part of Confucianism."[4] Huang identifies Wang as representing the *hsia* tradition, or righteous knight-errantry, which Wang expressed both in national defense and in righting local wrongs. Conservative Confucians have always been ambivalent about the *hsia* tradition, as it operates outside of official channels and relies on martial rather than moral suasion, but Huang once again showed his progressive views: "Ssu-ma Ch'ien's biographies of knights-errant, in comparing local knights-errant and independent scholars, endorsed the local knights-errant; in comparing knights-errant of humble origins and high official knights-errant, he was critical of the humble. The times change, and now those who cherish a measure of righteousness have no choice but to take the path of knight-errantry."[5] Thus Wang represents a reproach to the literati, most of whom capitulated to their alien masters, and at the same time Huang points out Wang's naturally refined manners in spite of his lack of formal education. Huang was seeking a perfect balance, and criticized reliance on unprincipled military might: "Ssu-ling went too far in emphasizing military might and relied on thugs and ruffians."[6]

This balance between *wen* (the cultural) and *wu* (the martial) could be achieved either by unlettered men acquiring principles and polish or men of letters acquiring honesty and courage.

Lest all this talk of knight-errantry and Confucian scholars lead us to stereotypical views of China's cultural isolation, Huang, writing in the mid 1600s, already showed an awareness of the decisive role of Western artillery in foreign and domestic political conflicts. Huang reports that superior fire power enabled the Europeans to extract an apology from the Japanese for killing missionaries in 1651, and even figured in the suppression of loyalist resistance in the South in 1659. However, although unlike Ch'i Chi-kuang, Huang does not explicitly comment on the relationship between martial arts and military science, he does make it clear that the survival of the martial spirit relied on the righteous knight-errant, and knight-errantry relied on the martial arts.

The word ch'i does not appear once in the Huangs' writings on Wang Cheng-nan and the Internal School, yet it is both central to Huang's philosophy and to our conception of what makes t'ai-chi ch'üan and the internal arts unique. In a long commentary on the phrase, "I cultivate my great ch'i" in the *Mencius*, (*Mencius*, Chap. 9 "Kung-sun Ch'ou") Huang summarizes his views:

Between heaven and earth there is nothing but one monadal ch'i that produces humankind and all things. Human beings are endowed with a portion of this ch'i when they are born. The mind is the most subtle aspect of the ch'i, or what is commonly understood as the intellectual ch'i that rises to the top. The mind is in constant motion, and the principles underlying that motion are called "intrinsic nature" (*hsing*). . . . When it moves in a orderly fashion, it is called "principle" (*li*). Principle is invisible, but manifests in the ch'i; intrinsic nature is invisible, but manifests in the mind. The mind is ch'i. When the mind is not cultivated, it becomes wild and uncontrolled, meaning that its movement has become disorderly. Cultivating the ch'i is cultivating the mind. Some speak of cultivating the mind, but this is something very difficult to grasp. However, cultivating the ch'i involves powerful movements and morning breathing exercises that give us a concrete path to follow. Buddhism's belief in "purifying the mind to reveal our original natures" holds that by not producing ch'i we can discover the source of ch'i. This is what they mean by "our original appearance," "our prenatal existence," and "stilling the mind by silence." When it comes to meditation, this is simply obstructing the ch'i and preventing its movement. They seek the original nature of the mind outside the ch'i, but I do not know what kind of "mind" they are purifying, or what kind of "intrinsic nature" they are revealing. Although the body consists of ch'i in motion, the moving ch'i must have a ruler. That ruler is not outside the movement, but is the principles underlying the movement. Looking at it from the point of view of change, we call it "movement"; looking at it from the point of view of the unchanging, we call it the "ruler." When those who would cultivate their ch'i preserve the ruler, blood and ch'i are transformed into reason; when the ruler is lost, reason is transformed into blood and ch'i. There is a very fine line between the two.[7]

Some of the salient features of Huang's statement include the unity of man and nature, the unity of mind and body (ch'i), and the unity of principle (li, tao) and matter (ch'i). All of these non-dualities, of course, are based on the universality of ch'i. Huang attempts to break through the age-old debate concerning the priority of mind or ch'i cultivation by denying any essential qualitative distinction between mind and body. There are distinctions of function and refinement but not of nature. T'ai-chi theory is also based on this assumption of fundamental body/mind unity. According to Huang, will (chih), intelligence (chih), and righteousness (i) are also functions of the ch'i.

Keeping his focus chiefly on Wang's prowess and character, Huang omits any reference to health benefits in relation to Internal School practice, but again, this does not mean that he ignored the issue in his other writings. Huang expresses his views on Taoist health practices in an epitaph written for Wan Tsu-sheng:

> Wan Tsu-sheng had been frustrated for many years in the civil service bureaucracy. In his later years, he became a disciple of the Taoist Lang Yao-sheng and learned Hsüan-men ch'i-kung from him. He practiced faithfully for several decades and suddenly announced that he had attained the goal. As I survey the intellectuals of the Chin and Yüan dynasties, most of them leaned towards Taoism, and thus the Ch'üan-chen Sect was very popular. Today Buddhism prevails, and the followers of Lao tzu are very few, but greedy and clever individuals who attach the name of Lao tzu to the alchemical arts are as numerous as hemp and bamboo. . . . Wan was fanatically devoted to his master Yao-sheng and truly believed he held the secret of immortality. However, the followers of the Ch'üan-chen Sect are secondary in importance and cannot escape the criticism of Confucian scholars. Nevertheless, Wang Lung-hsi's breathing exercises and Lin Lung-chiang's occultism have always been used by the Confucian scholars to strengthen their faculties and perhaps may be considered a legitimate method.[8]

Huang gives qualified endorsement to Taoist body/mind disciplines for the purposes of health maintenence, but rejects the notion of immortality. Again, he is a true Confucian in supporting self-cultivation that strengthens us for social engagement, but condemning those practices that lead to fantasy and obsession. The *Art of the Internal School* offers little detail on the internal energetics of the art, but Huang Pai-chia's account of Wang's *Archery Method* gives us a glimpse into the depth of his thinking:

> There is a method for the body, the hands, the feet, and the eyes. Although archery is performed with the hands, in reality

it is rooted in the body. Avoid puffing out the chest or leaning backward. Crouch low in Branch Stance, just as in the hand form. The body should be motionless, and the arm concealed. The power of the shoulder, elbow, waist, and legs should be concentrated. The arm must be straight and horizontal. The left hand, left eye, and left shoulder, as well as the right shoulder and right eye should be aligned. When drawing the bowstring and releasing the arrow, the left hand should not attempt to play an active role, but allow the right hand to do all the work. The toes of the left foot and the heel of the right foot should be coordinated with the shoulders and hands above. The eyes must not focus directly on the target, for if the eyes are on the target, then the hands and target will not be in alignment. When taking one's position, the toes of the left foot should point directly at the bull's-eye. If the body's posture is correct, the hands and feet will be coordinated. When drawing the bow, if the right eye focuses on the left hand, one will never miss.[9]

The *Art of the Internal School* is short on principles and internal energetics, but one can see from this passage that there was an awareness of whole body mobilization, eye-hand coordination, and discrete energies for different part of the body.

What about Chang San-feng, the "Taoist alchemist" who is credited in the "Epitaph" with founding the Internal School art and adopted by late Ch'ing-early Republican t'ai-chi ideologues as patriarch of their art? A number of scholars beginning in the 1930s have questioned the role of this legendary figure in initiating a transmission that continued unbroken down to t'ai-chi ch'üan, but few have questioned Chang's role in the Internal School. In this whole discussion, it might be instructive to learn Huang's views on Taoist alchemy:

Lin Chao-en's teachings emphasized Confucianism as the root, Taoism as the elementary level, and Buddhism as the highest teaching. However, looking at his personal practice, his pursuit of the elixir of immortality and spiritual liberation is very close to the heterodox school of Taoism. Hsieh Chao-che of Zhejiang said that Wan died insane. His disciples reported that in his later years he seemed to have an obstruction in his chest, was unable to speak, and did not know the names of his own servants. This is the disaster of alchemy.[10]

Huang was one of the most skeptical and critical scholars in all of Chinese intellectual history. Given his antipathy to alchemy, what are we to make of his naming the "Taoist alachemist" Chang San-feng as the progenitor of the Internal School? He may have simply reproduced the genealogy related by Wang Cheng-nan and recorded by Kao Ch'en-ssu, who drafted the biography that formed the basis of the "Epitaph," or he may have fabricated or altered the raw material to allegorically express his strategy for surviving and eventually defeating the Manchus. At very least, we can see that Huang, or even Wang for that matter, were not promoting or practicing Internal Boxing for "Taoist" reasons. The promoters of t'ai-chi ch'üan in the late Ch'ing and early Republican period were also good Confucians, responding to political and social realities. It is perhaps safe to say that Huang adopted Chang San-feng as a symbol of Chinese culture and nationalism. Late Ch'ing-early Republican t'ai-chi ideologues consciously identified with this narrative, as their project no less than Huang's was the salvation of the nation. We need to separate the issues of the philosophical orientation of the art, which has definite Taoist leanings, from the historical motivation for its practice. With the collapse of the social imperative in China at the close of the twentieth century, Chang San-feng has reemerged, but in the current incarnation it is for commercial or cultural rather than nationalistic propoganda purposes.

In my *Lost T'ai-chi Classics from the Late Ch'ing Dynasty* I suggested that for Huang, Wang represented a Chuang tzuesque "knack master," or in Western romantic terms, a "noble savage." But examining Huang's lesser known writings reveals another dimension of his view on skill, one that is consistent with his anti-Taoist, anti-intuitionist philosophy. Any discussion of the Confucian versus Taoist approaches to skill (*chi* 技) is inevitably framed by Confucius' "the gentleman is not a tool" and Lao tzu's "through skill we approach the tao." Huang compares the Confucian and Taoist approaches to skill using Mencius and Chuang tzu as their respective spokemen. Huang assumes that his readers are intimately familiar with both texts, but a bit of background would not be out of order here. The *Mencius* says: "Carpenters and wheelwrights can be given compasses and squares, but they cannot be given skill,"[11] and in the *Chuang tzu* we find:

> Those who understand the tao do not speak, and those who speak do not understand the tao. . . Lun Pien, an old wheelwright, said to Duke Huan [who was earnestly reading the classics]: "Let me use my own occupation as an analogy. In making wheels, if my hands are too slow they will be lax and unsteady; if they are too fast they will be stuck and blocked. When I cut neither too fast nor too slowly, then there is natural harmony between hand and mind. I cannot communicate this in words, but there is a very subtle truth involved. I cannot even explain it to my own sons, and they are unable to carry on my art. So, although I am seventy years old, I am still engaged in making wheels. The ancients, together with that which they cannot possibly transmit in words, are both dead. In this way, what you Duke are reading is nothing but ancient garbage.[12]

Huang was very concerned that Mencius not be interpreted to mean that skill, and especially morality, are innate and will spontaneously blossom when stifling convention and education are removed. Reacting strongly against Taoist antinomianism, Huang says:

> When the compass and square are thoroughly mastered, then skill is born. Skill resides within the compass and square. This

is what [*The Great Learning*] means when it says that progress comes from study. When the student abandons morality and tradition and seeks knowledge above the realm of human life, this is tantamount to abandoning the compass and square in search of skill. Chuang tzu's analogy of the old wheelwright encourages us to give up benevolence and righteousness in search of the tao, to give up "garbage" in search of what the ancients "could not transmit in words."[13]

Huang feared that Taoism and Ch'an Buddhism encouraged disdain for social responsibility and led to self-indulgence. He could not accept the view that the pursuit of wisdom or skill was simply a matter of deconditioning, or social deprogramming. Liberal Confucians like Mencius taught that human nature was essentially good, and goodness needed only nurturing; conservative Confucians like Hsün tzu taught that human nature was essentially selfish and needed control. As much as Huang opppsed Confucian cant and hypocricy, he associates himself here with the need for standards and training. To be sure, the *Art of the Internal School* emphasizes that freedom flows from skill, and skill flows from training.

In addition to such monumental works as the *Ming-i tai-fang lu, Sung Yüan hsüeh-an,* and *Ming ju hsüeh-an,* Huang wrote hundreds of inscriptions, biographies, and epitaphs. His "Epitaph for Wang Cheng-nan" is one of the most intensively researched and frequently repro-duced martial arts documents in China. It is the earliest source on the cleavage between internal and external schools and was adopted by late Ch'ing-early Republican t'ai-chi exponents as their "Genesis" on origins and genealogy. Previous historians have either accepted or denied the notion of a linear transmission from the Internal School down to t'ai-chi ch'üan. However, a survey of Huang's miscellaneous writings reveals many insights that have not heretofore entered the debate. It is interesting to see, for example, how the epitaphs, tributes, biographies, and poems dedicated to martyrs of the anti-Manchu resistance movement are echoed two hundred years later in the writings of the Wu brothers of Yung-nien. In fact, Huang Pai-chia and Wu Yü-hsiang, redactor of the t'ai-chi classics and founder of the Wu (Hao) style, are an intriguing pair: both dropped out of the examination system, both turned to business pursuits, and both had encounters with martial arts masters that resulted in their receiving critical transmissisons and in recording key documents for posterity. It is also interesting that Huang Tsung-hsi and Huang Pai-chia identify the school of brute force with Shao-lin, when Mao Yüan-yi in his *Wu-pei chih* (published 1621) says: "Shao-lin excels at combining hard and soft and never tries to overcome an opponent with brute force. Ch'eng Tsung-yü [author of *Shao-lin kun-fa ch'an-tsung*] in studying Shao-lin staff eliminated the soft and learned only the hard."[14]

T'ang Hao was unable to find any trace of the Internal School during his investigations in Ningbo. Actually, as early as the *Ch'ing-shih kao* (Draft history of the Ch'ing dynasty), compiled during the early Republican period, the editors reproduced the Huangs' biographies of Wang Cheng-nan, but when it came to any direct relationship between the Internal School and t'ai-chi ch'üan, they simply say: "During the middle of the Ch'ing period, t'ai-chi ch'üan appeared in Hebei. They say that their art originated with Wang Tsung-yüeh of Shanxi, however, their postures and principles are different in many respects from Pai-chia's account of the Internal School. By the end of the Ch'ing, t'ai-chi ch'üan became very popular."[15] Recent attempts to establish the Wu-tang Mountains as the true cradle of t'ai-chi ch'üan and to rival Ch'en Village and Yung-nien as holy places has led to a great deal of spurious scholarly activity, but a few discoveries worth looking at as well. Of all the names mentioned in the three Internal School documents, only Chang Sung-hsi, Tan Ssu-nan, Wang Cheng-nan, and Huang Pai-chia can be verified as historical figures in available sources. Tan, Wang, and Huang were all contemporaries living in the 1600s, and Chang Sung-hsi is said to have lived during the Chia-ching reign (1522–1566), two hundred years before Ts'ao Ping-jen's 1735 biography of him in the *Ningbo Gazetteer*. This biography has been the basis for the projection of a "Sung-hsi School"

(*Sung-hsi p'ai*) by Wu-tang promoters and used synonymously with
"Internal" or "Wu-tang." We do not know the sources for the *Gazetteer*
biography, but it appears to have drawn on the "Epitaph for Wang
Cheng-nan" for the Chang San-feng connection and details on the
Internal School and on local Ningbo legends for anecdotes about his
life. All of this makes it a very unreliable source. In 1988 Chang Ju-
an published an article announcing the discovery of an earlier source
for Chang Sung-hsi, a biography written by Shen Yi-kuan (1537–
1615) entitled "Biography of the Martial Artist Chang Sung-hsi" (Po-
che Chang Sung-hsi chuan). Shen says he wrote the biography based
on interviews with Chang's students, and many of the anecdotes,
and even some of the language, parallel those in the *Ningbo Gazetteer*.
Although Chang Ju-an is anxious to exploit this new source to bolster
the existence of a "Sung hsi-School" and silence critics like T'ang
Hao and Matsuda Ryuchi, ironically the biography itself makes no
mention of Chang San-feng, the Internal School, or any soft-style
principles. According to the Shen biography, Chang was a native of
Ningbo and was most likely there at the same time that Ch'i Chi-
kuang made it his headquarters in the mid sixteenth century. Why,
then, does Ch'i make no mention of "Internal Boxing" in his catalogue of styles, and why does the Shen biography describe Chang's
art generically, with no stylistic labels or soft-style philosophy?

Research in the written record is one approach to tracing historical
roots. A more anthropological approach is to conduct fieldwork in
order to uncover living traces of ancient traditions. Undaunted by
T'ang Hao's futile attempts to discover evidence of the Internal School
in Ningbo in the 1930s, Chang Yi and Ch'e Ming-kuei report in
1984 the discovery of contemporary practitioners of the Internal
School's "Six Paths" in Nanjing. Li Sung-ju and Li Chung-ch'i set
down the transmission in writing in 1972 and brought it to public
attention in 1983. They trace the transmission of the Six Paths back
to the Hsüan-te reign (1426–1439) of the Ming, filling in the more
than five hundred year gap between then and the present with a
wish list of famous folk heroes, including the "three heroes of the

South"—Kan Feng-ch'ih, Li Wei, and Teng Chung-shan—whose prowess is ascribed to knowledge of this form. Most of the postures and techniques correspond in their terminology with the contents of the *Art of the Internal School* of Huang Pai-chia. This means that it could be a reconstruction based on the existing written record, but of course does not rule out the possibility of an unbroken oral transmission. Interestingly, the author's of the article completely leave out the name Chang San-feng and all the rest of the *Art of the Internal School* lineage.

What the late nineteenth century framers of t'ai-chi ch'üan took from the Internal School was a lineage (Chang San-feng, et al), a strategy (softness overcoming hardness), and an ideology (Chinese nationalism). Early t'ai-chi ideologues—Kuan Pai-i, Sun Lu-t'ang, Hsü Lung-hou, Sung Shu-ming, Ch'en Wei-ming, Tung Ying-chieh, and Cheng Man-ch'ing—all spliced the Internal School and t'ai-chi lineages together. The name Chang San-feng does not appear in the Ch'en family or Wu/Li/Hao family manuscripts and is thus a product of the last days of the Ch'ing or early Republican period. In both t'ai-chi and the Internal School there is a self-conscious attempt to distinguish themselves from the hard school. The "Epitaph" states: "Shao-lin is famous for it boxers. However, its techniques are based on attacking the opponent." The "Wang Tsung-yüeh Treatiste on T'ai-chi ch'üan" states: "There are many other schools of martial arts. Although they differ in their postures, they are nothing but the strong overpowering the weak, the slow yielding to the swift. . . ." Huang Pai-chia tells us that the Six Paths was used to train strength and the Ten Sections Tapestry was used to train softness. This dual training also seems to have been a feature of Ch'en family training and even of early Yang and other styles. The "Epitaph" initiated the concept of two great schools—the external and the internal—and t'ai-chi ideologues in the late Ch'ing period seem to have revived and consciously associated themselves with the Wu-tang camp. This line may not have been so clearly drawn in the minds of Ch'en family practitioners. There are many political elements in the construction of the Internal School, and politics played a role in its adoption as progenitor for t'ai-chi ch'üan.

Huang, Wang, and the Internal School had the right patriotic pedigrees to serve as t'ai-chi's ancestors and as cultural standard bearers for China. The Internal School may or may not have been the biological parent of t'ai-chi, but t'ai-chi reached out to embrace the Internal School as an adopted parent. The Internal School, as projected by the Huangs, was Confucian in its nationalistic stance. However, as befits an agrarian empire, with a literati ruling class accustomed to defending itself against herding and seafaring peoples, it was also necessary to occupy the high moral ground by adopting an art that emphasized "overcoming movement with stillness" and allowing the opponent to strike the first blow. The "Epitaph" says that Chang was summoned by the Sung Emperor Hui-ts'ung (1101–1126), and it may not be a coincidence that this period, like Huang's own, saw China divided, with a barbarian Liao dynasty in the North. Similarly, the ploy of recruiting the Ju-chen (ancestors of the Manchus) to drive out the Khitans backfired, and the Ju-chen turned on the dynasty. Ch'i and Huang were preoccupied with China's inability to balance the *wen* (civil) and *wu* (martial), and both traced this to a defect in ruling class culture. This problem persisted down to the twentieth century, when t'ai-chi was being constructed to play a role in China's revival. The spiritual connection between the Ming-Ch'ing and Ch'ing-Republican transitions was pointed out by Wu Wen-chung, whose *T'i-yü shih* (History of physical education) states: "The late Ch'ing nationalist revolution was very influenced by them [anti-Manchu patriots Yen Hsi-chai (1613–1682), Wang ch'uan-shan (1619–1692), etc.] The righteous writings of Huang Tsung-hsi, Yen Hsi-chai, and other partriots were very influential at this time."[16] No less a figure than the father of the Chinese revolution, Sun Yat-sen, looking back to Huang's period, said:

> By the K'ang-hsi reign (1662–1722), the majority of intellectuals had already been coöpted by the Manchu government, and

therefore thoughtful, patriotic individuals realized they could not rely on the literati to keep the spirit of nationalism alive. Consequently they gathered together the lowly and homeless and entrusted the spirit of nationalism to these secret societies.[17]

Looking forward to his own time, Sun observed:

With China's adoption of Western armaments, the majority of Chinese have abandoned martial arts, resulting in the further weakening of individuals in society. . . . Our citizens are only interested in the most superficial aspects of the material culture of the West and discard our own traditional skills as useless.[18]

From Lu Hsün, China's foremost modern novelist and an astute critic of the national psyche, to Hu Shih, renaissance intellectual and Nationalist embassador to the United States, to Ch'en Tu-hsiu, co-founder of the Chinese Communist Party in 1921, there was unanimity across the political spectrum concerning China's declining power and the need to rekindle the martial spirit.

Huang Tsung-hsi, Huang Pai-chia, and Wang Cheng-nan inspired generations of patriots for their unbending spirit of resistance to foreign domination. Huang's account of the Internal School has also sparked scholarly controversies that have lasted from the beginning of modern historical research in Chinese martial arts in the 1930s down to the present. Second only to the Chang San-feng wars is the issue of the meaning of the "internal-external" dichotomy. The "Epitaph" is undisputably the locus classicus, but the text is far from unambiguous: "Now there is another school that is called 'internal,' which overcomes movement with stillness. . . . Thus we distinguish Shaolin as 'external.'" The three most common interpretations of the distinction between "internal" and "external" in the martial arts are: 1) Chinese versus foreign, 2) monks versus laymen, and 3) ch'i cultivation versus muscular development. As outlined by Huang Tsung-hsi, the Internal School was a revealed and discreet transmission, but it was adopted in the early twentieth century as a general framework for distinguishing hard and soft styles. Nevertheless, we may ask whether Shaolin is "external" because legend has it that Bodhidharma brought it to China from India, because Shaolin monks are "outside" of the family, or because the external school emphasizes an offensive strategy based on strength and speed? Comparing Huang Tsung-hsi and Huang Pai-chia's versions of Chang's creation myth, the former has Chang visited in a dream by the God of War, and the latter has Chang a Shaolin master who "reversed its principles." The text is ambiguous enough to support any of these interpretations, and it is difficult at this point to disqualify even one of them. Tsung-hsi's "attackers are effortlessly repulsed" and Pai-chia's "even a smattering of this art is sufficient to overcome Shaolin" may be ascribed to stylistic license, but also suggests an uncharacteristic lapse in objectivity.

The three primary sources on the origins of the Internal School, its characteristics and transmission, in chronological order are: Huang Tsung-hsi's 1669 "Epitaph for Wang Cheng-nan," Huang Pai-chia's 1676 "Art of the Internal School," and Ts'ao Ping-jen's 1735 *Ningbo Prefectural Gazetteer*'s "Biography of Chang Sung-hsi." These three are translated below.

Epitaph for Wang Cheng-nan

by HUANG TSUNG-HSI

Shaolin is famous for its boxers. However, its techniques are chiefly offensive, which creates opportunities for an opponent to exploit. Now there is another school that is called "internal," which overcomes movement with stillness. Attackers are effortlessly repulsed. Thus we distinguish Shaolin as "external."

The Internal School was founded by Chang San-feng of the Sung dynasty. San-feng was a Taoist alchemist of the Wudang Mountains. He was summoned by Emperor Hui-tsung of the Sung, but the road was impassable. That night he dreamt that the God of War transmitted the art of boxing to him and the following morning single-handedly killed over a hundred bandits.

A hundred years later, San-feng's art spread to Shaanxi Province, where Wang Tsung was its most noteworthy exponent. Ch'en Chou-t'ung received the art from Wang Tsung and taught it to his fellow villagers. In this way it spread to Wen-chou.

During the Chia-ching period, Chang Sung-hsi was the leading practitioner of this art. Sung-hsi had several disciples, among which Yeh Chi-mei (Chin-ch'üan) of Ssu-ming was the most noteworthy. In this way it spread to Ssu-ming. Among the Ssu-ming students who received the transmission of Chin-ch'üan were Wu K'un-shan, Chou Yün-ch'üan, Tan Ssu-nan, Ch'en Chen-shih, and Sun Chi-ch'a. K'un-shan transmitted it to Li T'ien-mu and Hsü Tai. T'ien-mu transmitted it to Yü Po-chung, Wu Ch'i-lang, and Ch'en Mao-hung. Yün-ch'üan transmitted it to Lu Shao-ch'i; Chen-shih transmitted it to Tung Fu-hsing and Hsia Chih-hsi. Chi-ch'a transmitted it to Ch'ai Yüan-ming, Yao Shih-men, Seng Erh, and Seng Wei. Ssu-nan's student was Wang Cheng-nan.

Ssu-nan had served as a military officer under Kuan Pai. After retiring from the army and returning home, he was very secretive about the subtleties of his art. Practicing behind closed doors, even his students were unable to catch a glimpse. Cheng-nan spied on him through a hole in the floor boards and got the general idea. Ssu-nan's sons were unworthy, and he lamented that after his passing there would be no one to carry on. When Cheng-nan heard this, he presented him with several silver goblets to be used for financing tea production. Ssu-nan was very moved by this gesture and gave him the whole transmission from beginning to end.

Cheng-nan was a very cautious man, and after receiving the transmission, never betrayed the slightest hint of it. He only used his art in the most dire emergencies. One night there was an incident involving a spy, and Cheng-nan was detained by the guards. He was tied to a pillar, and more than a score of men stood guard with a great deal of drunken revelry. Cheng-nan picked up a piece of broken pottery and secretly cut his bonds. Drawing a piece of silver from his bosom, he tossed it into the air, and all the men struggled to grab it. In this way he was able to escape. The men pursued him, but they stumbled about and fell to the ground, crawling on all fours and unable to stand. After covering a few miles, they lost him among the fields. The guards were still convinced that he was a criminal and surrounded him in great numbers. Wherever Cheng-nan struck he left wounded.

Once during his later years Cheng-nan was traveling alone, when he encountered some soldiers who tried to coax him to carry a heavy load for them. He begged to be excused, but they insisted. Cheng-nan waited until he reached a bridge and then threw the load over. The soldiers drew their swords and pressed him. Defending himself with bare hands, several of the soldiers were sent sprawling and dropped their swords with a clank. He threw their swords into a well, and by the time the soldiers retrieved them, Cheng-nan was far away.

In striking opponents, Cheng-nan made use of acupuncture points—death points, mute points, and vertigo points—just as illustrated on the bronze models of the channels. He once beat an incorrigible fellow, who as a result was unable to urinate for several days. Only after personally calling upon Cheng-nan and apologizing was he restored to health. A herd boy secretly stole the secrets of his art and used it to attack one of his companions, who immediately died. When Cheng-nan saw the body, he said: "This is only a vertigo point, and before long he will revive." Sure enough, this proved to be true.

Cheng-nan was a knight-errant and would avenge wrongs only when moved by real injustice. Once an old friend offered him money to avenge a wrong committed by the man's younger brother. Cheng-nan responded in no uncertain terms: "Do you take me for an animal?"

Cheng-nan's given name was Lai-hsien, his surname Wang, and his style Cheng-nan. He moved from Feng-hua County in Zhejiang to Yin County. His grandfather's name was Tsung-chou, his father's name Tsai-yüan, and his mother's maiden name Ch'en. For many generations they lived near East Bridge in the eastern part of the city. When Cheng-nan was born, they moved to T'ung-ao.

As a young man, Cheng-nan had an interview with Lu Hai-tao (Jo-t'eng). Hao-tao tested his abilities and gave him a post. Cheng-nan single-handedly undertook the work of several people and reported directly to the provincial governor. He carried out his duties unstintingly and was named to fill the post of company commander in Lin-shan. Ch'ien Chung-chieh (Kung-chien) appointed him to a higher military post.

After the military disaster, Cheng-nan vowed that until defeat was avenged he would maintain a vegetarian diet to express his dedication to this goal. Those who knew him were deeply moved.

Cheng-nan gave up his post and retired to his home. Those who admired his skill thought that because he was poor he could easily be compromised. The high-ranking military officers all paid their respects, but he was completely unaffected and ignored them. He continued to dig in the fields and haul manure as if unaware that he possessed a skill that could gain him an easier living.

One day Cheng-nan met an old friend who happened to share living quarters with the garrison commander. Just then Drill Master Yen Sung-chiang was instructing his troops in the martial arts. The drill master, relaxing and strumming the three-stringed lute, regarded Cheng-nan with his hemp headgear and coarse clothing as a nonentity. When his old friend mentioned that Cheng-nan was adept at boxing, the drill master, glancing sidelong at him said: "Is this true?" Cheng-nan modestly declined. The drill master, loosening his clothes and raising his eyebrows said: "How would you like to have a little match?" Cheng-nan once again declined. The drill master, taking him to be a coward, pressed him more forcefully, and so Cheng-nan had no choice but to respond. The drill master was thrown once, and when he requested another round, was thrown again with such force that blood streamed down his face. Thereupon the drill master bowed low and presented him with two rolls of fine silk.

Cheng-nan had no formal education, but was refined and cheerful in conversing with the gentry, with no hint of crudeness. Once I accompanied him to the T'ien-t'ung Temple. One of the monks, Shan-yen, was renown for his strength, and four or five men could not pin his arm. As soon as Cheng-nan touched him, he jumped back in pain. Cheng-nan said: "Nowadays people feel that the internal art lacks dazzle, and so they adulterate it with the external. For this reason the art is doomed to decline." This is why he consented to recording its origins.

Nine years have passed quickly since Cheng-nan died grieving for his son's death. Kao Ch'en-ssu wrote a biographical sketch and asked me to compose an epitaph. He was born in a certain reign year, 1617, on the fifth day of the third lunar month and died in a certain reign year, 1669, the ninth day of the second month. He was fifty-three years old. His wife's maiden name was Sun, and he had two sons. His oldest son Meng-te died a month before he did, and his second son's name was Tsu-te. He was buried on a certain day on the south side of T'ung-ao. The inscription reads:

Possessing the highest level of skill,
Yet he never abused,
Or prostituted it.
His devotion will be sorely missed.
Water is shallow and mountains old;
Who will look after this lonely grave?
May those who read this inscription
Learn from his life.

Art of the Internal School

by HUANG PAI-CHIA

Wang Cheng-nan was a master of two skills: one was pugilism and
the other archery. From ancient times great archers have been many,
but when it comes to pugilism, truly Master Wang was the foremost.

The external school of pugilism reached its highest development
with Shaolin. Chang San-feng, having mastered Shaolin, reversed its
principles, and this is called the Internal School of martial arts. Acquiring even a smattering of this art is sufficient to overcome Shaolin.
Master Wang Cheng-nan studied under Tan Ssu-nan and was the
only one to receive the full transmission.

In my youth I did not study for the civil service examinations and
was easily distracted. When I heard of Master Wang's reputation, I
hastened to his home and expressed my desire to study with him.
Master Wang jealously guarded his art and was extremely selective
in transmitting it. Nevertheless, he enthusiastically welcomed me
and transmitted his art. There were five types of students he refused
to teach: the treacherous, the belligerent, drunkards, loose talkers,
and the weak and clumsy. His home being too small, he instructed
me in the nearby Iron Buddha Temple.

There are a number of terms for the techniques in his art: long
fist, rolling chop, cross the heart, elbow presses gate, iron fan against
the wind, casting aside and seizing the fore, elbow the privates, bend
chest jab ribs, Emperor Shun's son throws himself into the well, cut
wrist press joints, sun shining through rosy clouds, black clouds covering the moon, monkey offers piece of fruit, bind elbow cover shoulder,
immortal with facing palms, bend bow take giant step, exchange
embraces of the moon, raise whip left and right, iron door bolt,
stringing fish on a willow branch, belly full of pain, hail of arrows,
picking up a piece of gold, double rack brush, diamond throw, two
hands push window open, leading a compliant goat, drawing out

hemp fiber, swallow raises cheeks, tiger buries its head, grasping the waist four times, and so forth.

There are a number of pressure point techniques: death points, mute points, vertigo points, coughing points, bladder, toad point, Jumping Round (huan tiao, GB-30), Pool at the Bend (qu chi, LI-11), throat lock, jaw dislocate, Union Valley (he gu, LI-4), Inner Pass (nei guan, PC-6), Three Li (shou san li, LI-10), and so forth.[1]

There are a number of errors to be avoided: lax and slow, crooked and hunched, tottering steps and protruding chest, stiff erectness and weak legs, floating elbows and jabbing fists, gyrating hips and bent waist, opening the gate and chasing shadows, simultaneously extending both hands, and so forth.

The most important principle of this art is practice. With practice comes mastery; there is no need to look around and imitate others. Simply be spontaneous in reacting to your opponent. Whether vertical, horizontal, back or forth, one is always in the right place at the right time.

Among the training methods are thirty-five hand techniques: chop, remove, jerk,[2] knock, lean, seize, press, rub, mow down, beat, shake, swing, release, sickle, grasp, encircle, support, snip, separate, provoke, bind, rush, hook, bridle, pounce, exchange, substitute, constrict, rise, topple, push down, issue, insert, pare, and bait.

There are eighteen footwork techniques: support stance, back support stance, stone roller stance, rushing stance, release stance, bent stance, stamping stance, hesitation stance, horseback stance, suspended horse stance, branch stance, immortal stance, body dividing stance, turn around stance, pursuit stance, pressing stance, diagonal stance, and twist flower stance.

All of these techniques are combined in the Six Paths and Ten Sections Tapestry. The secret transmission of the Six Paths is as follows:

"Arm thrust of the tutelary gods" is the highest technique.
"Dipper gate" locks securely, making you a hero.
The immortal stands up in the posture "facing heaven."

Execute "embrace moon," showing no mercy.
"Brandish whip" to the left and right, and the opponent
    cannot touch you.
Pound fiercely and seize forcefully, with "both wings flapping."

This is the Ten Sections Tapestry:

Stand up and assume mountain tiger posture.
Turn around and take three rapid pursuit steps.
Raise two swords and restrain your steps.
Execute rolling chop, advancing and retreating three times.
Divide the body with cross hands, while taking three rapid
    pursuit steps.
After raising sword and hacking, return to post.
Twist fist, roll step, then assume original posture.
With rolling chop, retreat, returning to your first path.
Move in, following closely, and advance without break.
Execute rolling chop and return to original position with
    flying steps.
Golden cock stands on one leg, drawing the bowstring tight.
Straddle the horse, maintain the four horizontals, and gaze
    to both sides.

Because the words to these verses are hermetic and difficult to
remember, I have undertaken to annotate them, lest they be forgotten.
The Six Paths are annotated as follows:

"Dipper Gate": The left arm hangs at one's side, and then the fist
    thrusts upward directly in front of the body. The right hand, bent
    and horizontal, faces outward. The two fists, opposite each other,
    form the Dipper Gate.

"Branch Stance": The right foot extends at an angle in front of the
    ankle [of the left foot], while the weight rests on the left foot
    behind the ankle [of the right foot].

"Drawing Out Hemp Helter Skelter": Starting from the left fist, the right hand hooks in and out with two fingers. The right foot follows the right hand, circling in and out in front of the left foot, making little stamping steps and returning to branch stance.

"Arm Thrust": This is what is meant by "long fist." The right hand, with palm facing forward, thrusts out in long fist. While the left hand lies over the breast, repeat four extensions of long fist. With the feet in branch stance, follow the long fist, turning left and right. When executing long fist, the hand should be vertical, with the back of the hand facing in. If the back of the hand faces outward, this is an error and exposes one to injury.

"Immortal Faces Heaven": The left hand in long fist attitude reaches behind the right ear, chops down to the left, and then rests over the breast. The left foot pivots to the left. The right hand reaches behind the left ear and then chops downward toward the right, and hooking up, is placed over the back of the left hand. The right fist is placed directly in front of the nose as if in the attitude of "facing heaven." The heel of the right foot steps out directly forward, pointing to the outside and bearing the weight. This forms an angle with the toes of the left foot, resembling the character *ting* 丁 . This is the "stance of the immortals." All stances should be low; high stances are an error.

"Embracing the Moon": The right foot takes a giant step backward and to the right. Allow the left foot to rotate to the right, and at the same time assume "horseback stance." The two fists are held horizontally with the palms facing each other in the attitude of "embracing the moon." Now rotate the forward hand and return to "dipper gate." The feet assume "branch stance" as you execute long fist four times. Draw in the left and right fists and cross them tightly over the chest, with the backs of the hands facing out; the right hand is on the outside and the left on the inside, while the two elbows grip the ribs.

"Brandish Whip": The left foot rotates to the rear, leaving the right foot in front and the left behind. The right foot then advances forward in "pursuit stance." The right hand attacks with the back (*yang*) of the hand facing forward and the inside (*yin*) of the upper arm facing up with the elbow extended straight out and the arm bent, that is, part of the arm is horizontal and part vertical, like a carpenter's square. The left hand is drawn back and rests over the ribs. As you come to a halt, turn to the other side. The left hand now attacks with the back of the hand facing out and the inside of the upper arm facing up, as the left foot advances forward, as on the other side.

"Wicked Pounding": The left hand is extended horizontally, with the inside facing out. The right hand moves backward, circling around to the left palm. The right foot, synchronous with the right hand, moves forward to a point behind the left foot.

"Forceful Seizure": The right hand moves to the rear as you turn the body and chop directly down. At the same time, the right foot rotates to the rear, while the left foot is lifted off the ground. The left fist thrusts downward to a point over the left knee in "suspended horse stance." This specifically defeats Shaolin's "embrace earth, dig gold bricks" and similar techniques. The right hand seizes the left elbow, and the left hand rises vertically from inside the right hand. The left foot advances forward in "pressing stance," while the right foot moves forward at the same time. The feet now return to "branch stance," while the hands assume "dipper gate."

"Two Arms Flapping": Both hands flap as the feet rotate to the right into "horseback stance." The two fists, held horizontally and with the inside (yin) facing the body, are brought close to the chest. First brush outward with the right hand held horizontally and extended straight like a wing. Now draw it back to the chest and repeat the movement with the left hand.

The "Ten Sections Tapestry" annotations are as follows:

"Crouching Mountain Tiger Posture": Assume "dipper gate" posture. From "branch stance" the foot rolls out to the right into "horseback stance." The two fists, horizontal and with palms facing in, touch the breast.

"Three Rapid Pursuit Steps": Release the right hand, and as the body rotates, the left hand extends in long fist posture, as in the Six Forms. The only difference is that the Six Forms uses the "branch stance," and when the body rotates, the right foot remains in front. Here, however, we use advance, retreat, and hesitation steps through three cycles of advance.

"Two Swords and Hesitation Steps": The left arm hangs at your side and then comes up straight in front of you with a fist. The right hand, in a bent horizontal position, opens to the outside, crossing the left hand on the inside. The feet slow to a halt.

"Rolling Chop, Advancing and Retreating Three Times": The forward hand moves downward in a wiping movement, while the rear hand chops forward. Repeat this, advancing three times and retreating three times. All chopping techniques are round above, straight in the middle, and round below, just like an axe.

"Divide the Body with Cross Hands": The two hands are in contact with the breast. Now release the left hand, and as it moves outward, the left foot follows it. The right hand extends outward, executing three repetitions of long fist. The right hand is in contact with the breast and is then released outward. The left foot pivots, while the left hand executes three repetitions of long fist.

"Raise Sword, Hack, and Return to Post": The right hand again is crossed, with the left hand on the inside. "Hack" uses the "rolling chop" technique, as before. Turning only the face, chop three times. Now using the right hand, turn the body.

"Twist Fist Roll Step": The fist sinks downward, and the left hand extends slightly. The right hand extends from below and advances upward. Both hands are held palm outward. The left foot follows the left hand; the right foot follows the right hand in rotating. Do not turn the face during the two twists.

"Rolling Chop, Retreat, and Return to First Path": The left hand executes three chops as the body turns around and retreats.

"Advance, Following the Opponent Like a Sheath": The left hand, held horizontally, touches the breast. Release the hand so that it moves outward until straight. The right hand forms a fist and covers the wrist of the left hand. The left foot follows the left hand, as one executes "hesitation step" and turns the body around. The right hand now is held horizontally in front of the breast and proceeds as with the left hand.

"Execute Rolling Chop and Return to Original Position with Flying Steps": After the right hand chops, the right foot rotates.

"Golden Cock Stands on One Leg, Draw the Bowstring Tight": The right hand chops again as the left foot rotates. The left fist punches down from above. In "suspended horse stance," the left foot advances half a step; following this, the right foot returns to "branch step" as in the Six Path's "fist thrust, suspended horse stance."

"Straddle Horse, Maintain Four Horizontals, Gaze to Both Sides": This is the same as the Six Path's "two wings flapping." Return to "dipper gate," turn the body, and execute "straddle horse, flap wings."

The Six Paths and Ten Sections Tapestry are very similar, but in general the Six Paths train the bones to make them tight, whereas the Ten Sections Tapestry trains them to be relaxed after they are already strong.

When Master Wang saw that I had written this down, he laughed and said: "I have practiced this art for a lifetime and yet still find it difficult to recall, but you have made it so simple. Nevertheless, from now on the art will never reach the highest perfection."

What Master most emphasized, what he was proudest of, and what set his apart from common arts was the Coiling Chop. Martial artists consider the chop to be the most important technique. There are basically four types of chops: rolling chop, willow leaf chop, cross chop, and Thunder God chop. Beyond these, Master Wang invented the coiling chop, which enables one to counter a chop with a chop. Thus from Master's long practice wisdom was born, and from analysis came enlightenment. Hence he was able to accomplish this unique innovation.

During the period that I practiced in the Iron Buddha Temple, the training was arduous and intense. Following training sessions, Master Wang and I sometimes had a few cups of wine and strolled about the garden. When the moon rose over the mountains, we would listen to the murmuring of the flowing stream, and Master would reminisce about old times. In discussing current events, he would often wax passionate. Because I also studied spear, broadsword, double-edged sword, and battle-axe, he said: "After your hand techniques are perfected, the weapons are not difficult. Such and such a place contains the spear techniques, such and such a place the sword or axe techniques." He left nothing out, even including marching and battlefield formations. He also said: "I have no successor; I will teach you everything I know." At that time I was hot-tempered and impetuous, looking up to Sui Yang and Po Chi. I believed that the affairs of the world could not be entrusted to those contemptible Confucian scholars, but required men who could jump on their horses and slay the enemy, jump off and capture the king.

This is the only life worth living. However, by that time, the southwest was already pacified, and the southeast was also quiet. The whole country was at peace, truly a time better suited to the simple farmer than the great warrior. My father noticed that I was headstrong and unrestrained, and fearing that I become simply a young ruffian, directed me to prepare myself for the civil service examinations. I could also see that the family fortunes were declining, and even if I perfected my art, it would be useless. I thus came to regret having studied the martial arts. Giving up my former ambitions, I devoted myself to practical affairs. I picked up my umbrella and briefcase and sought counsel with Ch'en K'uei-hsien, Ch'en Chieh-mei, Fan Kuo-wen, Wan Chi-yeh, Chang Hsin-yu, and others. We had all assembled in Ningbo, and when Master Wang came to the city, he visited me in my studio. Coming around to the subject of martial arts, he very earnestly said: "In the martial arts it is not a question of practicing many techniques, but of perfecting a few. When you have achieved perfect mastery, then the Six Paths will be seen to have infinite applications. Among these are the yin and the yang, and although there are only eighteen techniques, their transformations may be multiplied to forty-nine." He also said: "A technique like "twisted flower pounding" may be executed to the left, right, middle, forward, and backward. Do not just focus on one side." He also said: "Martial arts proceed from the complex to the simple. From the seventy-two throws (e.g., long fist, rolling chop, cross hands over heart, etc.) and twenty-five hand techniques (e.g., chop, remove, jerk, knock, lean, etc), we derive eighteen (i.e., the eighteen techniques contained in the Six Paths). From these eighteen we derive twelve (reverse, exchange, twist, shift, roll, remove, pull, knot, kneel, sit, beat, and seize), and summarizing these twelve, we may keep in mind "respect, relentlessness, directness, power, and precision." At that time I was preoccupied with my literary studies, and although I forced myself to listen, it was not with the old enthusiasm. Moreover, Master Wang, now suffering poverty and illness, was dejected, jaundiced, and completely exhausted.

Master Wang has been dead for only seven years, and already local bandits have joined together and swarm over the highways. The bones of the innocent cover the countryside. Now if we could find but one Sang I,[3] it would be sufficient to eliminate the bandits. In the midst of this, the examination candidates are still mumbling over their books behind closed doors. The local authorities have issued some orders for defense, mutual aid, and the like, while the young scholars collect some clichés about the "unity of soldiers and peasants," as if this was sufficient to solve the problem.

The well-known Ch'in Shih-lu said: "If our helping hand were here now, he would show them!" These words express how much he lamented that Master's bones lay underground.

Alas, Master is gone forever! Now I truly miss my studies with Master Wang. I dare not claim that this constitutes a strategy for delivering the nation from its oppressors, but as for local defense, perhaps like Fan Ch'ang-sheng and Fan Ya, we might protect our own villages and neighborhoods. I thought this could be a possible solution. How could it have turned out that bandits fill the world, and here we stand holding our umbrellas, looking about at the chaos with nowhere to hide? Once I regretted wasting my time studying with Master Wang, but now I regret only my former regrets.

I was the only one to receive the transmission of Master's art, but now as I have neglected this knowledge, this art is already all but lost. How could I bear this? For this reason I have recorded a fraction of it in hopes that those who take an interest will be able to grasp it from this. Although detailed plans for Chu-ko Liang's famous war machine have been available for three thousand years, who has been able to make use of them?

Biography of Chang Sung-hsi

from the *NINGBO PREFECTURAL GAZETTEER*

Chang Sung-hsi was a native of Yin County in Zhejiang Province. He was an expert martial artist and a disciple of Master Sun Shih-san. According to him, his art originated with Chang San-feng of the Sung dynasty. San-feng was a Taoist of the Wu-tang Mountains. Emperor Hui-tsung summoned him, but the way was impassible and he could not proceed. That night he had a dream that the God of War transmitted the martial art to him, and the following morning he single-handedly killed more than a hundred bandits. From that time on his skill spread throughout the world. After San-feng, the art was transmitted to Ssu-ming during the Chia-ching reign (1522–66) of the Ming, and Sung-hsi was its foremost exponent.

In his conduct, Sung-hsi was as courteous as a scholar, treating others with the utmost respect and humility. Whenever approached to teach his art, he would always make excuses and retire. At that time, the Shaolin Temple was renown for its boxers, and when China was invaded by Japanese bandits, the monks were recruited to drive them out. A group of some seventy monks heard of Sung-hsi's reputation and came to Yin County to see him. Sung-hsi, however, refused to come out to receive them. Shao-nien encouraged him to meet them, and he found all the monks sparring upstairs in a wine shop. When they saw him, they suddenly looked very sober, for they knew it was Sung-hsi and they invited him to have a match. Sung-hsi folded his arms and just sat there. One monk charged him and attempted a kick, but Sung-hsi slightly turned his body, raised his hand, and sent the man flying through space like a bullet. Falling from the upper story of the building, he nearly died, whereupon all the monks were scared into submission.

Once Sung-hsi and Chu Shao-nien went to the provincial capital, and Chu managed to confine him there for a month. Lo Pai said: "Now you cannot escape, and I wonder if you could give us a demonstration." Sung-hsi had no choice and so he had Shao-nien raise a pile of round stones weighing several hundred *chin* each. He said: "I am a useless old man of seventy years. Let me give you a good laugh." Raising his right hand he came down with a slicing chop, and three stones were split in half. This illustrates the miraculous level of his skill.

Sung-hsi had three or four disciples, among whom Yeh Chin-ch'üan was the foremost. Chin-ch'üan's disciples were Wu K'un-shan, Chou Yün-ch'üan, Tan Ssu-nan, Ch'en Chen-shih, and Sun Chi-ch'a. K'un-shan transmitted the art to Li T'ien-mu and Hsü Tai. T'ien-mu transmitted it to Yü Po-chung, Ch'en Mao-hung, and Wu Ch'i-lang. Yun-ch'üan transmitted it to Lu Shao-ch'i; Chen-shih transmitted it to Hsia Chih-hsi and Tung Fu-fu; Chi-ch'a transmitted it to Ch'ai Hsüan-ming, Yao Shih-men, and to Buddhist monks Seng Erh and Seng Wei. Ssu-nan's disciple was Wang Cheng-nan. Cheng-nan's given name was Lai-hsien, and he exemplified righteousness above all things. He conducted himself with courtesy and reserve, never showing off his skill.

There are two schools of the martial arts: one is the External School and the other is the Internal School. The most popular of the external styles is Shao-lin. Their art emphasizes striking techniques, along with jumps and leaps. However, a momentary loss of balance can be exploited by an opponent. Sung-hsi transmitted the orthodox tradition of the Internal School. Its techniques emphasize defense, only attacking when the opponent is in serious trouble, and then with devastating consequences. The Internalist gives his opponent no opportunity to take advantage of and thus remains superior. In striking opponents, they use pressure points, including vertigo points, mute points, and death points, each of which can be attacked with varying degrees of pressure. Their most secret teaching was the five word transmission: "Respect, relentlessness, directness, power, and precision," which was only given to initiated disciples. These five words do not themselves represent applications, but are the means by which the techniques reach the highest level, just as military strategists speak of "benevolence, honesty, intelligence, courage, and strictness."

4

Ch'ang Nai-chou's Writings on Martial Arts

Introduction

Unlike Ch'i Chi-kuang and Huang Tsung-hsi, Ch'ang Nai-chou is not a towering figure in Chinese history. In fact, he is not even a towering figure in Chinese martial arts, and his name is only known to a handful of martial arts historians. Nevertheless, although the style he created is all but extinct, he left behind a body of writings on martial arts unrivaled for their depth and subtlety in the premodern period. Even more tantalizing are the twenty odd phrases shared between Ch'ang and the "t'ai-chi classics" and the most evolved example of the marriage of martial arts, medicine, and meditation. The existence of t'ai-chi language and theory in the body of a radically different art means that we must rethink the evolution of t'ai-chi ch'üan in terms of diffusion rather than transmission.

Ch'ang's writings are strictly technical and free of political overtones. Living a century after the Manchu conquest and another century before its overthrow, he had the psychic space to fully develop the internal aspect of the martial arts. Ch'ang Nai-chou was a native of Sishui County, Henan, and lived during the Ch'ien-lung reign (1736–1795) of the Manchu dynasty. Like Huang Pai-chia and Wu Yü-hsiang, Ch'ang was born into a gentry class family. He held the entry-level "annual tribute student" degree, but his older brother Shih-chou held the highest, or *chin-shih*, degree. The *Sishui Gazetteer* gives no dates for Ch'ang,[1] but the biography of his brother Shih-chou tells us that Shih-chou won his *chü-jen* degree in 1738 and his *chin-shih* in

1742. This gives a firm chronological frame. The *Gazetteer* tells us that Nai-chou suffered from spermatorrhea and at the age of more than thirty began to practice meditation and martial arts. He studied with fellow Sishui native and Spirit Boxing master Chang Pa of Hulao, while at the same time immersing himself in the *I ching* and unnamed "ancient martial arts manuals." The *Gazetteer* reports that Ch'ang's tread shattered paving stones, and his tap cleaved stone table tops. He wore a shirt dyed with coal dust, and after practice his whole body was stained black. The biography does not specifically mention his participation in bandit suppression, but the biographies of his students describe their exploits in defending their hometowns against White Lotus, Nien, and local rebels. The only three legitimate excuses for gentry class individuals to practice martial arts were health, national defense, and bandit supression. The *Gazetter* mentions health as Ch'ang's initial motive and goes on to glorify his feats, but Ch'ang's writings themselves actually hold the distinction of being our first received documents presenting the martial arts as a practice for realizing the tao. The *Gazetteer* biography gives no other clues into his sources or influences, and significantly, makes no mention of t'ai-chi ch'üan or the Ch'en family.

Ch'ang's own preface states that his teacher Chang Pa of Hulao began to study martial arts at the age of thirty and that he, Ch'ang Nai-chou, studied from his boyhood. His older brother urged him to desist, but Nai-chou continued to search far and wide for a true master. After ten years in the wilderness, he met Yen Sheng-tao of Loyang and began to progress. After ten more years he learned Forty Techniques Character Boxing, and synthesizing and augmenting this, created his own system. It would seem that Forty Techniques Character Boxing was the skeleton of his style, but unfortunately we have no record of this art. Hsü Chen, pioneering martial arts historian in the 1930s and redactor of Ch'ang's writings, follows the "Author's Preface" version of events and ignores or did not consult the *Gazetteer*. In his "Preface" to *Ch'ang Nai-chou's Writings on Martial Arts*, Hsü Chen reports an alternative version of Ch'ang's lineage that takes Yü Jang as his first teacher. Hsü also relates some anecdotes about fanciful feats of lifting stone columns, demolishing two foot thick stone steps, walking on water, wall climbing, and the like, but personally maintains some skeptical distance. Less sober scholars like Ch'en P'an-ling[2] in the 1930s and Li Ch'eng[3] in the 1980s embroider this scant record with interesting apochrypha and combine it with Ch'en Hsin's claim of Ch'ang's visit to Ch'en Village and apprenticeship there. Li Ch'eng even weaves a tale of Ch'ang Nai-chou and Ch'en Chi-hsia trading secrets and teaming up to rid the world of bandits. Explaining the source on which he based his published edition of Ch'ang's works, Hsü states that fifth generation grandson Ch'ang Te-p'u taught the family art to fellow Sishui native Yüan Yü-hua, who first made the material public in Shaanxi. Feng Ch'ao-ju obtained a copy from Yüan and showed it to Hsü, who edited it and brought it out as a book in 1932. It is on this book that the present translation is based.

As befits Ch'ang's epithet "scholar martial artist," his "Twenty-four Character Form Manual" is a rich literary composition. Surveying technical terminology in all styles of martial arts, we see three basic principles at work: the literal, the poetic, and the mnemonic. Ch'ang combines single character mnemonic titles with eight highly allusive seven character verses, drawing on aphorisms, mythology, history, alchemy, occultism, the natural world, and Buddhism, and taking us on an encyclopedic tour of Chinese history and culture. Looking at the very first set of postures, for example, he uses the familiar myth of the peach of immortality and three figures from history and legend: Emperor Wu of the Han, Tung-fang-Shuo, and Queen Mother of the West. The *Classic of Mountains and Seas* (Shan-hai ching) tells us that in the middle of the sea is a mountain with a winding path of three thousand *li* leading to a great peach tree growing at its peak. Emperor Wu (157–87 BCE) is famous for his obsession with finding an elixir of immortality in his old age. The first line describes the delicate touch called for when first making contact with the peach. The second line alludes to plucking the peach, which requires a certain amount of force. The third and fourth lines compare martial arts applications to climbing a peach tree to reach the fruit. The fifth and sixth lines bring in Tung-fang Shuo, a wise minister who used humor to advise Emperor Wu during the Han, and the verse ends with a tribute to the Queen Mother of the West, a goddess who is also associated with immortality.

Sishui County is located directly across the Yellow River from Wen County, the home of Ch'en Village and the birthplace of t'ai-chi as we know it today. Ch'en Hsin, the first Ch'en family member to publish a comprehensive form and theory manual for the Ch'en style, says in the biography of his ancestor Ch'en Chi-hsia: "One day Chi-hsia was painting images of the Buddha in the Ku-sheng Temple when someone pushed him from behind. Chi-hsia threw the man, and on asking his name, learned that it was the famous martial artist Ch'ang Nai-chou"[4] In his biography of Ch'en Chung-shen, Ch'en Hsin tells us that during the Hsien-feng period (1851–1861) "bandits" (Taiping rebels) overran Sishui, but were afraid to cross the river into Wen County because of the superior defenses organized by Chung-shen. Ch'en Hsin's *Illustrated Manual of Ch'en Style T'ai-chi ch'üan* (Ch'en-shih t'ai-chi ch'üan t'u-shuo) is prefaced 1919, after three generations of Yang's had already won fame and fortune with the art, and the work is a transparent attempt to bring the glory back to Ch'en Village. Ch'en Hsin is not a reliable source on historical events in Ch'en Village, and well reasoned articles have appeared regarding the authenticity of the poem attributed to Ch'en Wang-t'ing, inaccuracies in the family biographies, and possible interpolation of the words "t'ai-chi ch'üan" in the form manuals T'ang Hao examined during his research there. Some intriguing structural, linguistic, and content parallels between Ch'ang's writings and Ch'en Hsin's *Illustrated Manual* bear further study, but at this stage do not allow us to say definitvely either that Ch'ang influenced Ch'en Village, or vice versa. Strictly on the basis of geography, it is not unreasonable to imagine that Ch'ang Nai-chou visited Wen County, however, Ch'ang's form and that of Chenjiagou and nearby Zhaobaozhen bear no resemblance to each other, and there is no written trace of Ch'ang's highly evolved theoretical teachings in Ch'en Village from the eighteenth century. In Ch'ang Nai-chou we have found a missing link, but the two ends of the broken chain are still too far apart to be perfectly mended.

Remembering that the "t'ai-chi classics" were unknown in Ch'en Village, we are compelled to ask how it is that the t'ai-chi classics and Ch'ang's writings have so much in common? In the form that they are most commonly seen today, the first classic is that attributed to a "Wang Tsung-yüeh of Shanxi." Unfortunately, there is no reliable historical evidence of this figure, but the language and principles Ch'ang shares with this text are too striking for them not to have a common source or spring from a common theoretical matrix. One's first impression of Ch'ang's writings is that although a collection of short essays, they add up to a book-length exposition of a martial art, compared to the half dozen or so pages of heterogeneous and variously authored texts that constitute the "t'ai-chi classics." Reacting to the theoretical similarities of the two bodies of writing, T'ang Hao says: "In discussing martial arts, although Ch'ang is not as concise as Wang Tsung-yüeh's "Treatise on T'ai-chi ch'üan," the principles are very similar."[5] Hsü Chen, the modern redactor of Ch'ang's writings, lists a number of prominent parallels between the two and concludes: "That Ch'ang also discovered the same principles as t'ai-chi proves how excellent his selections were."[6] Why do they make t'ai-chi the standard by which Ch'ang is measured, and why do they not consider that Ch'ang or his mentors may have been the source for these principles? Is it because Ch'ang's was a dead art and t'ai-chi, having already reached wide popularity, they were committed to promoting it as a national prescription and symbol; or was it because both T'ang and Hsü were married to Wang Tsung-yüeh and locked in a battle with each other to prove or disprove that Wang brought t'ai-chi ch'üan to Ch'en Village? Looking at evidence for the historicity of Wang versus Ch'ang and the scope of their respective writings, an objective historian today would be obliged to regard Ch'ang as a far richer vein for tracing the development of soft-style martial arts theory in the mid-eighteenth century.

Like the "Wang Tsung-yüeh Treatise," *Classic of Pugilism*, and "Epi-taph for Wang Cheng-nan," Chang Nai-chou defines and creates a distinctive identity for his art by making critical references to other arts. Ch'i Chi-kuang considered all styles to have their strengths but to be partial; Wang/Huang contrast their "internal" art with the "exter-nal"; the t'ai-chi "Treatise" speaks of "numerous other schools"; and Ch'ang warns against both "common arts" and "decadent gentry," who disapprove of martial arts study. There are no mythological references in Ch'ang's transmission. This is not to say, however, that there is no mystery. Between his own preface and the *Sishui Gazetteer*, we have the names of several teachers, but nothing about what they taught or how to account for the detailed internal energetics, unique in the history of Chinese martial arts literature. The fact that he does not mention Wang Tsung-yüeh or t'ai-chi ch'üan is also significant, given that his base of operations, northern Henan, is precisely where Li I-yü's "Postscript" claims the Wu family "salt shop classics" were found and T'ang Hao's "Bookstall classics" say Wang was active. This, however, is something that is more encumbant on t'ai-chi ch'üan to explain than on Ch'ang.

My *Lost T'ai-chi Classics from the Late Ch'ing Dynasty* presents in chart form the specific textual parallels between Ch'ang Nai-chou's writings and the t'ai-chi classics, so I will not repeat them here, but rather discuss a number of shared general principles. First is the priority of ch'i development: "The Twenty-four Character Form is about nothing but ch'i, and every posture must emphasize ch'i." To locate this ch'i we must look to what Ch'ang calls the tan-t'ien (as in the t'ai-chi classics), and also a series of synonyms—the "hsü-wei point," "heavenly root," "gate of life," or "t'ai-chi." This last is the only context in which Ch'ang uses the term "t'ai-chi," and it does not, of course, refer to a martial art, or even to a state of yin/yang equilibrium, but to the specific point just below the navel, com-monly called the tan-t'ien. In discussing the movement of ch'i in the body, his analytical tools parallel those in the t'ai-chi literature: yin and yang, full and empty, hard and soft, and the five phases. The

central theme of his whole work is ch'i development, and the word
appears in virtually every line of his text. At the very outset, Ch'ang
enters the age-old debate in Chinese self-cultivation circles concerning
the *wen* (spiritual) versus *wu* (physical) approaches to ch'i development.
The *wen* methods emphasize sitting, emptying the mind or visualization, and gentle breath regulation. Ch'ang places martial arts in the
service of the *wu* method to harmonize the physical body, regulate
the ch'i in the organs and channels, and produce the golden elixir of
the inner alchemists. What the inner alchemy tradition calls the
"original yang," and the medical tradition calls the "original ch'i,"
Ch'ang calls the "central ch'i."

Ch'ang says: "Those who practice my tao will at the highest level
be able to 'revert to the root and return to the source, transcend the
mundane and ascend into heaven' and at very least strengthen their
bodies, eliminate illness, and achieve longevity." This echoes the
same language employed in countless treatises on ch'i-kung and sexual
practices. Using the standard symbols and formulas of inner alchemy,
he explains that when the yang-ch'i of the ming-men moves forward
and upward, and the yin-ch'i of the heart moves down, and the two
meet in the "central palace," then ch'i coalesces and power is born.
We do not see such an explicit and detailed grafting of the goals and
methods of inner alchemy onto the martial arts until the *T'ai-chi fa
shuo* attributed to Yang Pan-hou in the late Ch'ing or Cheng Man-
ch'ing in the late 1940s. The first step in self-realization is ch'i cultivation, and the first step in ch'i cultivation is ch'i circulation. As in the
familiar medical model, each inhalation and exhalation drives the
ch'i through one circuit of the five viscera, and in one day it makes
a complete circuit of the viscera and bowels via the twelve channels.
This circulation takes place naturally, but can be actively promoted
and blockages removed by movement practices.

Ch'ang's movement method, and the theory underlying it, contrasts
sharply in one respect with that of t'ai-chi ch'üan and is unlike anything I have encountered in other martial arts or ch'i-kung practices.
As in the medical and macrobiotic models, Ch'ang considers the

posterior aspect of the body yang and the anterior yin, but then says
that bending forward (flexion) causes the yang-ch'i of the governing
vessel (tu-mai) and all the yang channels of the back to "enter" the
anterior aspect of the body. Bending backward (hyperextension) causes
the yin-ch'i of the controlling vessel (jen-mai) and all the yin meridians
of the anterior aspect of the body to "enter" the posterior aspect of
the body. The circuit of jen-tu circulation established with breath
and visualization through microcosmic orbit meditation is promoted
here by rhythmic backward and forward bending. Yin-yang interaction
is also encouraged by left-right rotation, opening-closing, diagonal-
sideways, and rising-falling movements. All but the backward-forward
bending are found in t'ai-chi body mechanics, which stresses "erect
posture as if suspended from the crown of the head." Continuous
ch'i flow requires that yin movement flow into yang movement, and
vice versa. As in t'ai-chi ch'üan, the priority is continuous whole-
body ch'i flow, and Ch'ang considers the movement from yin to yin
or yang to yang to be a prescription for stagnation.

    Where does power come from? For Ch'ang, proper body mechanics
is the foundation for ch'i flow, and ch'i flow is the prerequisite for
power. The goal of body mechanics—alignment of head, hands, and
feet—is whole-body integration, which together with synchronization
produces power. With the flexion of the twelve major joints of the
appendicular skeleton, the ch'i will also move superior-inferior,
anterior-posterior, or medial-lateral. For martial arts applications, it
requires unified ch'i of the whole body to be mobilized and issued
through one point. From the ming-men to the extremities there are
many opportunities for blockages. In order to avoid the negative
side-effects of softness (dissipation of the ch'i) or of hardness (con-
gealing of the ch'i), the two must be balanced. Assuming a posture
and mobilizing the ch'i is the "soft" aspect of application, and landing the blow is the "hard."

    Whole-body ch'i circulation and mobilization is the macrocosmic
circuit, but Ch'ang also outlines a number of microcosmic manifesta-
tions of the ch'i. The ch'i of the organs and of opening and closing

body movements is reflected in changes in facial color and expression. This is an example of the unity of internal states and external signs, and is a far cry from grimacing to frighten opponents as seen in "common arts." The ch'i also circulates in the "three points"—head, hands, and feet—depending on the attitude of the head, weight distribution in the feet, and the leading edge in the hands. The alignment of the "three points" is especially critical in issuing energy, and as in t'ai-chi, Ch'ang emphasizes the need for an open circuit from foot to hand. Another aspect of ch'i development is "ch'i absorption," which takes place during four movement circles—left, right, forward, and backward—and involves a show of effort in the brows, nose, and lips, together with forceful inhalation.

Self-defense applications, too, are explained on the ch'i level. Ch'ang's strategy of waiting until the opponent's ch'i is already commited to a definite course, and then beating him to the punch before he can block or retreat, is precisely the same as in the *Art of the Internal School* and the "t'ai-chi classics." The alternative to "borrowing" ch'i that the opponent has already issued is "seizing the ch'i," so that the opponent is effectively straight-jacketed and can never launch an attack. These strategies require a subtle sense of the opponent's ch'i in addition to our own. Issuing ch'i is a three step process, according to Ch'ang, and includes concentrating the ch'i, withdrawing the ch'i, and then releasing it. This is the concrete explanation for "mobilize the ch'i with softness and land the blow with hardness." Briefly touching on pressure point techniques, Ch'ang emphasizes the need to be mentally focused and to focus the power of the whole body on one point.

For beginners in his art, Ch'ang makes a number of specific recommendations that are closer to those of t'ai-chi ch'üan as we know it today than any other premodern art. He advises adopting a middle stance at first, and later, high and low stances. He recommends practicing the postures first in order to perfect body mechanics, and then by avoiding force and working slowly and in a relaxed manner, ch'i will naturally develop. His call for relaxing the shoulders, sinking the elbows, keeping the front foot straight and rear foot angled, not overextending the front knee, and keeping the head aligned with the body are all in complete accord with the classics or any t'ai-chi manual today.

If there are many striking commonalities between Ch'ang and the t'ai-chi classics, there are also some notable contrasts in the area of mechanics. T'ai-chi stresses maintanence of vertical alignment at all times, under the principle of "suspension from the crown of the head," whereas Ch'ang's form features frequent trunk flexion and hyperextension. The second major difference is that the t'ai-chi classics emphasize maintaining the weight on a single foot and avoiding double-weightedness, whereas Ch'ang twice specifically demands that "the weight of the body rest directly in the middle of the two feet." The third difference is that most t'ai-chi styles call for placing the foot flat or heel first, whereas Ch'ang's footwork specifically forbids flat placement and requires plantar flexion, with the toes touching down first. Fourth, one of the hallmarks of t'ai-chi practice is "relaxing the chest and raising the back," whereas Ch'ang flatly contradicts this, calling for "opening the front and closing the back." Fifth, Ch'ang's calling for isolated elevation or lowering of a single shoulder or hip violates the horizontal alignment typical of all t'ai-chi styles. Sixth, the emphasis on the role of the waist in t'ai-chi, though not contradicted in Ch'ang, is all but absent, except for one short verse passage devoted to the role of the hips. Seventh, "sticking and following" are specifically mentioned in Ch'ang, and "interpreting energy" is implied, but these are minor themes compared to their central importance in t'ai-chi. Ch'ang's received writings mention no form of push-hands or partnering practice, but stylized push-hands as we know it today is also not spelled out in the t'ai-chi classics. What we have, then, is two arts that share nearly identical theory, reveal fundamental differences in mechanics, and look nothing alike. This allows us to focus in on what is really unique in t'ai-chi ch'üan. In juxtaposing the two traditions, we can see that what makes t'ai-chi ch'üan unique vis-a-vis Ch'ang's art is not so much its internals as its mechanics, and in this respect the most important distinguishing features are erect posture and single-weightedness. The gap narrows considerably, however, if we compare Ch'ang's teachings, not to the t'ai-chi ch'üan of the "classics" or to normative Yang family works, but to Ch'en style t'ai-chi as described by Ch'en Hsin. In his *Ch'en-shih t'ai-chi ch'üan t'u-shuo*, Ch'en Hsin says:

"Not leaning or inclining does not refer to the physical body, but to a natural centeredness of the spirit. . . . If we combine this with bending forward and backward, flexing and extending, we will achieve a completely unified method. . . . Although the body may depart from the vertical, the vertical still exists internally; we must not be dogmatic. . . . Although the body executes leaning postures, the central ch'i circulating internally is naturally without unevenness"[7]

When it comes to the issue of "double-weightedness," Ch'en Hsin neither explicitly forbids it like the t'ai-chi classics, nor prescribes it like Ch'ang Nai-chou, but whether judging from the *T'u-shuo* illustrations, early twentieth century photographs of Ch'en Fa-k'e, or current Ch'en style practitioners, "double-weightedness" is seen in nearly every posture. Thus Ch'en explicitly disassociates himself from a strict construction of the verticality found in Yang and other styles.

Ch'ang Nai-chou's
Writings on Martial Arts

edited by HSÜ CHEN

Central Ch'i

"Central ch'i" is what the classics on attaining immortality call "primordial yang," or what in medical terms is called "original ch'i." Because it dwells in the very center of the human body, it is called central ch'i in martial arts terminology. Central ch'i is prenatal true monadal ch'i. Through spiritual cultivation it becomes the inner elixir; through martial cultivation it becomes the external elixir. However, the inner elixir is always dependent on the external elixir for its formation; this is because movement and stillness are each the root of the other. Proper cultivation naturally results in forming the immortal fetus and returning to the primordial state. Common scholars do not understand the source of central ch'i and think by simply moving their hands and feet they can penetrate the primordial mystery. This is impossible. From the moment of birth, human beings rely on prenatal spirit to transform into ch'i and on the accumulation of ch'i to transform into essence. When father and mother mingle their essences, they take shape in the hsü-wei point [tan-t'ien]. The hsü-wei point is located directly opposite the umbilicus in the front and the kidneys in the rear. It moves rapidly up or down, left or right, but never forward and backward, or leaning and inclining. It occupies the very center of the human body. It is called the "heavenly root," the "gate of life," or what the *I ching* calls "t'ai-chi." The "true yin and true yang" are both stored therein, and the spirit relies on it.

The spiritual brightness of this ch'i expresses itself as the spirits of the five viscera: the spirit of the heart, the *hun* soul of the liver, the mental reflection of the spleen, the *p'o* soul of the lungs, and the seminal essence and will of the kidney. All of these are sustained by it. The breath relies upon it: the inhalation extracts the ch'i of heaven and earth, and the exhalation exudes the ch'i of the five viscera. When we exhale, the ch'i travels from the ming-men to the kidneys, to the liver, to the spleen, to the heart, and finally to the lungs; when we inhale, the ch'i travels from the lungs to the heart, to the spleen, to the liver, to the kidney, and finally to the ming-men. The circulation of the twelve channels and fifteen network vessels is also closely related to this. The channels and network vessels are the pathways of the ch'i and blood. With each exhalation, the ch'i and blood advance three inches, and with a complete cycle of inhalation and exhalation, they advance six inches. People breathe 13, 500 times in one day and night, and the ch'i advances 810 *chang* (8,100 feet). The yang travels twenty-five degrees, and the yin travels twenty-five degrees, for a total of fifty degrees in one day and night. It circulates throughout the whole body, and from the viscera and bowels issues forth into the channels and network vessels. From the channels and network vessels it enters the viscera and bowels. In this way, the two forces (yin and yang) are generated, and thereafter the kidney and bones. The kidneys are associated with water, and water is able to produce wood. The liver belongs to wood and generates the sinews. The sinews are attached to the bones. In this way, the liver is generated and the sinews develop. Wood is able to produce fire, and the heart belongs to fire and governs the blood vessels. Fire is able to produce earth. The spleen belongs to earth and generates muscles and flesh. Earth is able to produce metal. The lungs belong to metal and govern the skin and hair. In this way, the lungs are generated, and the skin and hair develop. The five viscera and six bowels are generated and develop in an orderly sequence, and the physical body comes into being. Thus from the true monadal ch'i they miraculously come together and are formed. This is the aggregation of ch'i. It completes the body and abides within it. From the one comes two, and the two revert to one. We cannot escape this principle for a single moment. This is also true for the martial arts. Training the body unifies our external form; training the ch'i solidifies our internal aspect. When we are as strong and firm as iron, we naturally develop an indestructible golden elixir body. In this way, we transcend the common, enter sagehood, and attain the highest level. If it is said that an enemy does not fear us, this is of little significance.

The Entering and Support of Yin and Yang

Training the physical form is nothing more than yin and yang. If we fail to understand yin and yang, how would we know where to begin our training? The governing vessel (du mai) described in the classics on immortality traverses the midline of the back and commands all of the yang channels. The controlling vessel (ren mai) traverses the midline of the belly and commands all of the yin channels. Therefore, the back is yang, and the belly is yin. The two channels meet below at the perineum (hui yin, CV-1) and above at the frenulum (duan jiao, GV-28). One is in the south and one the north, just like the first (tzu) and seventh (wu) terrestrial branches, or like the trigram Kan (water), that occupies the very center of the north and the trigram Li (fire), that occupies the very center of the south. These are fixed and do not change. Bending forward is a yin posture and allows the yang ch'i to enter. It benefits the governing vessel, guides the ch'i of all the yang channels, and reverts to the upper front aspect of the body. Bending backward is a yang posture and allows the yin ch'i to enter. It benefits the controlling vessel, leads the ch'i of all the yin channels, and reverts to the upper rear aspect of the body.

The Entering of the Yang and Connecting with the Yin, and the Entering of the Yin and Connecting with the Yang

The back is yang, and when we bend forward, the governing vessel connects with the controlling vessel. That is, the yang crosses over and enters the yin, so that the yang and yin combine. The belly is yin, and when we bend backward, the controlling vessel connects with the governing vessel. That is, the yin crosses over and enters the yang, so that the yang and yin combine. The yin urges the yang, and the yang urges the yin, round and round in a continuous circulation. This principle is used in all rolls and turns.

The Yang Enters and Supports the Yin
and the Yin Enters and Supports the Yang

When we bend forward, the yang ch'i enters, and if we do not lift up the yin ch'i, there will be imbalance on the yang side, and we will suffer from pulling and falling forward. When we bend backward, the yin ch'i enters, and if we do not lift up the yang ch'i, there will be imbalance on the yin side, and we will suffer from pushing and falling backward. Therefore, when executing forward bending postures, we must quickly follow up with backward bending postures to avoid imbalance on the yin side. When the yin arrives, the yang reverses, and when the yang arrives, the yin reverses. Without leaning or inclining, without excess or deficiency, make your point and return to the origin: this is the essence of the method. When pushed to the point of bending, respond with extension; respond to extension with bending; respond to the high with the low; respond to the low with the high; respond to the sideways with the frontal; respond to the frontal with the sideways. It is just the same with the diagonal, the twisted, the rotating, or reciprocal. When practicing the postures in sequence, the yin and yang interact, and one naturally achieves perfect coordination of hand and mind without errors.

Both Yin and Yang Enter, and Both Yin and Yang Support

This is the sideways posture. When executing sideways postures, yin and yang each occupy one half. Therefore, when executing sideways postures to the left, the yin and yang of the right side both enter, and the yin and yang of the left side both support it. When executing sideways postures to the right, the yin and yang of the left side both enter, and the yin and yang of the right side both support it.

Yin and Yang Separately Enter,
and Yin and Yang Separately Support

This is the opening and closing posture performed with the arms horizontal. When opening the chest and closing the back, the yin ch'i separately enters the yang aspect. When opening the back and closing the chest, the yang ch'i separately enters the yin aspect. Because the posture separates to both sides, the ch'i splits from the center, separately entering and separately supporting.

Yin and Yang Rotate and Enter,
and Yin and Yang Rotate and Support

This is the horizontal wheel posture, the twisted posture, or the shaking posture. The postures rotate continuously, and the ch'i also follows without stopping. The yin enters and the yang separates; the yang enters and the yin separates. The process continues without interruption, rotating to the left and right. Yin and yang rotate, entering and supporting.

Yin and Yang Are Diagonally Imbalanced,
and the Entering and Supporting Cross

These are the diagonal, sideways, and bending postures. When we execute diagonal forward bending postures to the left, the yang ch'i rises from the lower right side of the spine up to the upper left side of the spine, diagonally entering the upper left front yin aspect. When we execute diagonal forward bending postures to the right, the yang ch'i rises from the lower left side of the spine to the upper right side of the spine, diagonally entering the right front yin aspect. This is used in diagonal splitting and intercepting hand techniques. When we execute diagonal backward bending postures to the left, the yin ch'i rises from the lower right side of the belly to the upper left side of the belly, diagonally entering the left rear yang aspect. When executing diagonal backward bending postures to the right side, the yin ch'i rises from the lower left side of the belly to the upper right side of the belly, diagonally entering the lower right yang aspect. This is used in scooping and raising hand techniques.

The Yin Enters and the Yin Supports,
and the Yang Enters and the Yang Supports

This represents postures that rise straight vertically or advance straight ahead without leaning or inclining. When the body is vertical and faces directly forward, the yang ch'i does not enter the yin aspect, and the yin does not enter the yang aspect. In this posture, each reverts to its original position. They meet above at the Hundred Convergences (bai hui, GV-20) point and below at the Gushing Spring (yong quan, KI-1) point. Yin and yang only enter and support at the two extremes.

Yin and Yang's Disorderly Entering and Supporting

This is the drunken posture. Drunken postures involve sudden movements to the front and back, bending forward and backward, advancing and retreating, diagonal and straight. The postures are irregular, and the ch'i follows the postures by entering and supporting. However, there is order at all times within this disorder. The yin and yang are not contrary to each other, for the disorder is actually not disorder at all.

The above generally describes the entering and supporting of the great yin and yang of the body. The back of the hand is yang, the outside of the arm is yang, and the three yang meridians traverse the outside of the hands and arms. The t'ai-yang channel of the hand begins on the back of the little finger; the shao-yang channel of the hand begins on the back of the ring finger; and the yang-ming channel of the hand begins on the back of the index finger. All of these travel along the outside of the arm. The palm is yin, the inside of the arm is yin, and the three yin channels traverse the inside of the hands and arms. The t'ai-yin channel of the hand ends at the inside of the thumb; the chüeh-yin channel of the hand ends at the inside of the middle finger; and the shao-yin channel of the hand ends at the inside of the little finger. All of these travel along the inside of the arm. The top of the foot is yang; the outside of the leg is yang;

and the three yang channels travel along the outside of the feet and
legs. The t'ai-yang channel of the foot ends at the second joint on
the top outside of the little toe; the shao-yang channel of the foot
ends at the second joint on the top outside of the fourth toe; and the
yang-ming channel of the foot ends at the second joint on the top
outside of the second toe.[1] All three of these channels travel along
the leg and end on top of the toes. The bottom of the foot is yin; the
inside of the leg is yin; and the three yin channels traverse the inside
of the foot and leg. The t'ai-yin channel of the foot begins at the top[2]
inside of the big toe; the chüeh-yin channel of the foot begins at the
top outside[3] of the big toe; and the shao-yin channel of the foot
begins at the little toe and passes through the yung-ch'üan point. All
three of these channels travel along the inside[4] of the leg. Although
there are innumerable methods of extending, bending, pointing, and
stepping with the feet, as well as bending, extending, raising, and
lowering the knees and hips, nevertheless the entering of yin and
yang are naturally constant. When the body is unified, the ch'i is not
pulled and dragged; when the body is not unified, the ch'i is obstructed and stuck. Experience this for yourself and do not overlook
the smallest detail.

The Transformation and Combining of Yin and Yang

The tao of heaven and earth is none other than yin and yang. The
transformation and combining of yin and yang arises naturally. Therefore, when stillness reaches its peak, there is movement, that is,
yang follows yin; when movement reaches its peak, there is stillness,
that is, yin follows yang. Applying this principle to the four seasons,
spring and summer follow fall and winter. When harvest and storage
reach their peak, sprouting and growth follow. After spring and summer, fall and winter follow. When sprouting and growth reach their
peak, there is harvest and storage. Yin must transform into yang, and
yang must transform into yin. This is the process of creation and
what allows life to go on forever. Human beings are endowed with
the ch'i of heaven and earth and thus are a microcosm of heaven and

earth. Can it be otherwise with these postures, which represent the transforming, combining, receiving, and continuing of yin and yang. Therefore, the high is yang and the low is yin; bending backward is yang and bending forward is yin; extending is yang and bending is yin; movement is yang and stillness is yin; the front is yang and the side is yin. High postures must drop to low postures, as yang transforms into yin. If high postures become even higher, to the point where they cannot go higher, there will be discontinuity, and the ch'i will not follow. Low postures must be raised to high postures; the yin is transformed into yang. If low postures become even lower, to the point where they cannot go lower, there will be discontinuity, and the ch'i will not follow. The same principle applies to bending forward and bending backward, flexing and extending, movement and stillness, side and front. If occasionally yin is once again transformed into yin, and yang into yang, this means that the one ch'i is not finished and needs to be encouraged to reach completion. It is not the case that complete yin transforms into yin or that complete yang transforms into yang. Understanding this, our transformation mechanism will exhibit definite postures, and continuing and descending will be associated with definite ch'i. There will be no conflict or error, pulling or dragging. The smoothness and speed of the postures and fluidity and flow of the ch'i will be uninterrupted. If there is an interruption, you will have to start all over, resulting in slowness and dullness.

The Three Points Are the Guideposts of the Ch'i

In all things, concentration brings order. This is because there is a controlling force and a commander. There may be a thousand heads and ten thousand tails, but they all revert to a single path. When an army marches according to the battle plan of a commander, and a family is managed according to the parent's standards, then there is cooperation, and they will fulfill their tasks. In training the body, ch'i, and the essence of movement, can we avoid getting to the bottom of the controller and root of ch'i? The head is the point of convergence for the whole body and controls the entire

body's ch'i. If the head is not unified, then the ch'i of the entire body
fails to enter. If you are in a forward bending posture, but the head
is tilted back, then the yang ch'i will not enter. If you are in a
backward bending posture, but the head is tilted forward, then the
yin ch'i will not enter. In forward bending postures to the left side, if
the head tilts to the right, then the yin and yang of the right half will
not enter; in forward bending postures to the right side, if the head
tilts to the left, then the yin and yang of the left half will not enter.
It is the same with backward bending postures. In vertically rising
postures, if the head retracts, then the ch'i from below cannot ascend; in vertically lowering postures, if the head projects outward,
then the ch'i from above cannot descend. When rotating to the
right, if the head turns to the left, then the ch'i does not enter the
right. When rotating to the left, if the head turns to the right, then
the ch'i does not enter the left. The three yin channels end on the
inside of the hand; the three yang channels begin on the back of the
hand. This is the pathway of the blood and ch'i of the arm when
executing split technique. With any disharmony in the flexing and
extending, gathering and separation of the fingers, or facing up and
facing down, extending and retracting of the wrist, then the upper
arm ch'i will not enter. If a horizontal yang hand is extended, but
the palm is reversed and hooked, the ch'i will not enter; if a horizontal yin hand is extended, but the palm is reversed and hooked, the
ch'i will not enter. If a yin hand moves down, but with the palm
drawn back, then the yang ch'i will not enter; if a yang hand thrusts
upward, but with the palm drawn back, the yin ch'i will not enter. If
a horizontal yin hand swings forward, but the wrist draws back, the
yin ch'i will not enter; if a horizontal yang hand strikes out, but the
wrist is drawn back, the yang ch'i will not enter. If a sideways hand
strikes straight ahead, but the hand drops, the ch'i will not enter. If
a sideways hand penetrates deeply, but the hand is drawn back, the
ch'i will not enter. Three yang channels end on the back of the foot;
three yin channels begin at the bottom of the foot. These are the
pathways for the blood and ch'i of the legs and hips. With any
disharmony in the toes, heel, edge, and sole of the foot, or the

extension, flexion, inside, or outside of the ankle, the ch'i of the body will not enter. If during backward bending postures, you stamp the foot or extend the toes, the yang ch'i will not enter. If during forward bending postures, you plant the foot with the toes in dorsi flexion, the yin ch'i will not enter. If during rising postures, you force the vertical and extend the toes, the ch'i will not rise; if during low postures, you sink excessively with the toes in dorsi flexion, the ch'i will not descend.

Alignment of the Three Points

Training the body is simply a matter of movement and stillness. When we move, the ch'i should be raised and not scattered; when we are still, we should be like an unshakable mountain. Only in this way are we totally free. By contrast, because they do not understand the alignment of the three points, common practitioners are unstable and inappropriate in their movement and stillness. When the three points are aligned, there is no problem of deviations to the east or west. If the three points are not aligned, then we are pulled and dragged this way and that, and we will inevitably suffer shaking and swaying. For example, in cross posture, with the left foot advanced and the right hand in front, the right hand should be precisely aligned with the toes of the left foot. The head too should be aligned with the right hand, and in this way the center and bottom form a straight line. When we avoid deviations, we enjoy stability. When the body is turned to the side with the right foot advanced and the right hand forward in conforming posture, the head is aligned with the right hand, and the right hand is aligned with the right foot. Everything else follows in similar fashion.

The Arrival of the Three Points

The arrival of the three points refers to movement and stillness arriving at the same time. There is no distinction of first and last, or fast and slow. When there is pulling and dragging, there is no arrival.

When your ch'i touches an opponent, although the contact is at just one point, the ch'i of that one point is in the whole body. If one point does not arrive, then there is pulling and dragging, and the ch'i of the body will not arrive. If in your practice you do not develop agility and speed, your attacks will not be sure and strong. This is the cause. In training your body, you must constantly pay attention to these three points, and then you will grasp the secret.

The Bending and Extending, Coming and Going, Landing of the Ch'i, Inside and Outside, Above and Below, and Front and Back of the Twelve Joints

The three points are the commanders of the ch'i and the places to which the ch'i reverts. People only know that these three locations should be strong and fierce, but they are not aware that the point of contact requires the whole body to be as strong as a rock. Only then will we not fear assaults or worry about our ability to defend ourselves. The reason one is firm and strong lies in the joints. The joints are spaces, or valleys, in the body where the spirit and intelligence converge. When spirit fills the joints, they are like iron or steel. Bend it, and no one can stretch it out; straighten it, and no one can bend it. The power of ch'i will then be perfect. The arm has three joints: shoulder, elbow, and wrist. The leg has three joints: hip, knee, and ankle. Combining the left and right sides of the body gives us a total of twelve major joints. The ability of the hand to grasp and the foot to step depend on these. This is just like filling a sand bag until it becomes very full. Although the contents are very soft, the bag becomes firm and hard. However, the movement of the ch'i follows the postures, whether they are forward or backward, inside or outside, above or below. For example, when we are sideways in an erect posture, with both hands scooping forward, the ch'i in the center of the elbows fills above, and the ch'i of the wrist is bent up. When both shoulders are dropped, and the knees are bent back, the ch'i fills the rear. When the ankles expand, the chi fills the front. When the hips are drawn in, the ch'i pushes internally. When we are sideways and both hands split downward, the ch'i in the center of the elbow fills in front, and the wrist ch'i fills below. When the forward shoulder drops down, the rear shoulder is raised up; when the forward knee is bent, the kneecap is pushed out; as the ankles bend they fill; when the rear hip bends, the rear knee extends backward; when the outside ankle extends and steps, the outside is raised backward; and when the hip is elevated, the body rushes forward. When both hands strike forward vertically from the side, the ch'i in the middle of the elbow fills in the center, and the ch'i of the wrist fills on the outside. When the shoulders drop, and the knee caps push forward, the ch'i fills in front. When the ankles are bent, the ch'i pushes in the rear. When the hips bend, and one executes four horizontals posture with the arms extended outward, the ch'i in the center of the elbow fills above, and the wrist ch'i fills within. When the shoulders are dropped, and the knees are spread apart, the ch'i fills the outside. When the ankles apply force on the inside and open to the outside. . . . The rest can be similarly deduced.

Moving the Ch'i

Making strong contact and being a fierce fighter depends on the ch'i of the whole body concentrating on one point. However, there are some practitioners who find that when they attempt a technique, the ch'i is not mobilized, or if it is mobilized, there is pulling, dragging, and inhibition. This is because they do not know how to move the ch'i. The ch'i in the human body issues from the ming-men, the source of ch'i. It expresses itself in the four limbs, the channels for the flow of ch'i. These should never be blocked or obstructed, and then we will be free of pulling and dragging, and our movements will be perfectly fluid and agile. Therefore, when ch'i from the top travels to the bottom, it should be made to enter the bottom without being dragged there; when ch'i from the bottom travels to the top, it should be made to enter the top without being stuck there. When ch'i from the front travels to the back, it should follow the back, and then the front will naturally enter. When the back ch'i travels to the front, you must regulate the front, and it will naturally go to the back.

When ch'i from the left travels to the right, you must pay attention to the right; when ch'i from the right travels to the left, pay attention to the left. If the hand strikes straight out, the ch'i should enter in front. If you do not restrain the rear hand and support the rear elbow, the ch'i will not enter from the back. When thrusting upward with the hand, if the bottom hand is not inserted and the shoulders are not dropped, the ch'i will not rise up from the ribs. When separating the hands, if the chest does not open, then the ch'i will not enter the rear. When bringing the hands together, if the chest does not open, the ch'i will not be contained in front. When rising straight up, you must hook your feet; when sinking straight down, you must retract the top of the head. The ch'i of the left hand is in the right foot; the ch'i of the right hand is in the left foot. In forward bending postures, sinking postures, and forward reaching postures, raise the heel of the rear foot. When dropping down, sit the arms; when raising up, lift the feet. When lowering and kneeling, do not bend the foot back in order to avoid pushing upward. When lifting the feet, do not stretch them out in order to avoid being pulled down. Expand and fill it. This applies to every posture. To sum up, the ch'i lands on one point, but it comes from many sources. If you open the source and free the flow, the path will be smooth and you will naturally avoid halting, dragging, and impediment.

The Complementary Relationship of Hard and Soft

When postures are without the three points, there is no landing; when the ch'i is without the three points, there is no completion. This is what is meant by the yin within yin transforming into yang and the yang within yang transforming into yin. Landing and completion take place where the ch'i gathers and the blood concentrates and returns. When it is appropriate to use the hard method, there is intermittent yin and yang, and thus the ch'i and blood flow smoothly. When it is appropriate to use the soft method, the same principle applies. If you use pure hard method, then ch'i fills the whole body, and there will be pulling, dragging, and inhibition, and there will be no fierceness at the point of impact. If you use pure soft method, then the ch'i scatters and is not concentrated. It has no place to revert to, and the landing point will not be firm and strong. You should be hard with softness, and then the ch'i will accumulate, but with no negative effects; you should be soft with hardness, and then the ch'i will scatter, but with no negative effects. Otherwise, you will not achieve the marvel of the complementary interaction of hardness and softness. Therefore, when hardness and softness are used adeptly, it is like a dragonfly just touching the surface of the water and immediately rising. Move the ch'i like a windmill that turns and rotates without stopping. In this way, the hard and soft are both in proper measure, and you will not suffer the ch'i being insufficient or inhibited.

The Five Phases in the Face

Anger stirs the liver and sound stirs the heart. The nose vents the ch'i, thus stimulating the metal of the lungs. The lips open and close, thus arousing the ch'i of the spleen. The knitting of the eyebrows projects ch'i into the kidneys. The ch'i of the five phases correspond with the five viscera. The liver corresponds to wood; the heart to fire; the spleen to earth; the lungs to metal; and the kidneys to water. Externally they open to the seven orifices. The eyes are the external orifice of the liver; the ears of the kidney; the mouth of the spleen; the nose of the lungs; and the tongue of the heart. Their essences flow into the eyes, and the five colors separate into the five mountain peaks. The forehead is the Southern Peak, and its color is crimson; the chin is the Northern Peak, and its color is black; the left cheek bone is the Eastern Peak, and its color is green; the right cheek bone is the Western Peak, and its color is white; the tip of the nose is the Central Peak, and its color is yellow. Further, what is produced on the sides of the eyebrows belongs to the wood of the liver; the pure ch'i passing through the nose belongs to the metal of the lungs; the eyes gather the essences and belong to the water of the kidneys; the tongue controls the sounds issuing from the tan-t'ien and belongs to the heart's fire; the lips control containment and belong to the spleen's earth. Generally, any movement can be reduced to simply flexing and extending, and the ch'i can be reduced to gathering and releasing. Similarly, the five phases reflected in the face must also be coordinated, and only then can we achieve the marvel of combined ch'i. Therefore, in gathering postures, the ch'i from the limbs and joints gathers in the Central Palace. The eyebrows should be knit; the eye sockets should be drawn in; the nose should open; and the lips should be pressed tightly together. The ch'i should be inhaled and the sounds swallowed. Thus the internal ch'i is gathered and concentrates. When executing expanding and dropping postures, the ch'i of the Central Palace issues into the limbs and joints. The eyebrows should be relaxed; the eyes should protrude; the nose should expand; and the lips should be parted. The ch'i should be exhaled, and the sound should be expelled. Thus the internal ch'i is released and the external form opens. If you pay attention to this and practice well, the internal ch'i will follow the external form and the external form will correspond to the internal ch'i. In this way, inner and outer are as one, and you will be as hard as a rock. When you use the method of attraction, first slap the opponent with the hand, then strike with the fist, and finally attack with rock bags and wooden bats. This proceeds from light to heavy, gradually attracting and gradually solidifying. In this way, you will never have to worry about the face being without ch'i. Common practitioners do not understand this and deliberately make grotesque faces to frighten opponents. Can these be considered enlightened gentlemen?

Color Changes of the Throat

This phenomenon occurs when one's practice has reached a very high level. The "true origin" being full and flourishing expresses itself outwardly from the inside. The ch'i accumulates and the blood concentrates, finally coalescing as one. Although human beings all share the same endowment, the ch'i that they receive is different, corresponding to the five natures of the five phases, the five forms, and the five colors. Therefore, those who are endowed with the ch'i of wood are sharp and slender in their form, joyful by nature, and crimson in color. Those who are endowed with the ch'i of earth are short and stout in their form, melancholy by nature, and yellow in color. Those who are endowed with metal ch'i are fair and beautiful in their form, sorrowful by nature, and white in color. Those who are endowed with the ch'i of water are fat and sleek in their form, fearful by nature, and black in color. When the ch'i has been trained to the highest level, then our practice will be perfected and the true ch'i full and abundant. When the ch'i is withdrawn and concentrated, the ch'i comes to rest and the blood accumulates. The blood is brilliant in color. When the ch'i and blood do not circulate, the muscles and skin follow the ch'i and stick to the bones. The true ch'i of the five forms fully manifests externally, each form expressing itself according to its endowment, and thus we have the five colors: green, black, red, white, and black. When these five appear in one individual, this shows that they possess all five ch'i. When the whole body is as cold as ice, this means that the true yang is completely withdrawn to the central palace and no longer expresses itself externally. Realizing this, you can understand that the flesh of the throat is influenced by the ch'i, and that the changes in color follow the ch'i. This is a natural phenomenon and has nothing to do with mysterious methods.

Accumulating Seminal Essence and Gathering the Spirit Are the Source of Ch'i Power

The spirit is the most subtle aspect of the ch'i; thus the spirit is transformed from the ch'i, but without the seminal essence, it will not transform. The ch'i in turn transforms into seminal essence. The birth of a human being is the bestowal of prenatal spirit that is transformed into ch'i. The accumulated ch'i is then transformed into seminal essence and finally forms the human body. After birth, we rely on the moistening fluids of postnatal water and grain to transform into seminal essence. The ch'i accumulates, transforms into spirit, coalesces in the elixir crucible, and gathers in the Yellow Court. It is immeasurably subtle and irresistibly powerful. It is the highest treasure of inner alchemy and the root of ch'i power. Thus ch'i is without form, belongs to yang, and transforms into spirit. Blood has substance, belongs to yin, and transforms into seminal essence. Spirit is formless and therefore it is subtle, immeasurable, and capable of infinite transformations. The seminal essence is substantial and therefore fills and coalesces. It is irresistibly strong. The spirit must rely on the seminal essence, and the seminal essence must attach itself to the spirit. When the seminal essence and spirit unite, the ch'i power is realized. One who understands the power of ch'i is spoken of as having the seminal essence and spirit to overcome all obstacles. Without seminal essence and spirit, there is no ch'i power. Martial artists who understand this strive to accumulate seminal essence and concentrate the spirit in order to strengthen the ch'i power. However, if they do not understand how to accumulate seminal essence or concentrate the spirit, they exhaust a lifetime of mental effort without results. How can they fail to realize that the spirit requires ch'i in order to concentrate, and the seminal essence requires the spirit to accumulate. If you want to experience accumulation of the seminal essence and concentration of the spirit, it is impossible without concentrating the ch'i. The method of concentrating it is simply to constrict the anal sphincter and contract the penis in order to raise the ch'i from the lower part of the body to the upper, so that it will not be drained off. At the same time, gather the ch'i of heaven and earth, inhaling with all your might and thus causing the ch'i from above to return to below and not be scattered above. When above and below are joined, they coalesce in the Central Palace, where the ch'i accumulates and the seminal essence coalesces. When the seminal essence coalesces, the spirit concentrates, naturally expressing itself outwardly from the inside, and we become everywhere hard and strong. This is the so-called internal solidification of the seminal essence and spirit spoken of by the virgin of Nanlin. However, one should practice constantly and establish a regular practice early, so that it can be applied in immediate situations and always be strong and solid. Otherwise, we are like a cannon without saltpeter and sulfur, or a bow without a string and arrow. When we are empty, there is nothing that can issue forth. It is impossible to expect someone in this state to have courage and speed or have the inexhaustible power of pounding seas and collapsing mountains. These are the essentials of training the body and ch'i. Guard these secrets and do not recklessly disclose them, lest you incur the wrath of heaven.

Moving the Ch'i

This is the method of knowing the proper pathways in hand-to-hand fighting. As soon as one hand is extended, the ch'i sticks to one side and cannot stick to all sides. When an opponent projects vertical force, it lacks horizontal force, and so I block horizontally. When an opponent projects horizontal force, it lacks vertical force, and so I block with vertical force. When an opponent attacks from above, it lacks force below, and so I challenge him below. When chopping down, there is no force above, and so I attack high. It is the same with diagonal, frontal, bending, and extending. This is the principle of attacking the empty and the unprepared. If my opponent uses this principle, I do not strike back, but simply change my hands, mobilize the two ch'i and then attack him. If he changes tactics again, I again change my hands, mobilize the three ch'i, and then attack him. This method of ambush is used when the opponent is unaware, but requires that I control his moving ch'i and cause him to be trapped. When the opponent's ch'i approaches, and while it is still in motion, I take advantage of this to smash him. Thus whether east or west, left or right, I meet his source everywhere. The critical point is just one move. As soon as he moves, I move immediately, thus depriving him of his source. If I wait for him to stop moving to initiate my movement, he will take advantage of my moving ch'i. The margin of error is no more than a hairsbreadth, and students must pay close attention. Let the opponent become fierce, for his ch'i will inevitably become unbalanced. It is natural that if there is fullness in one place, there is emptiness in another. The vertical blocks the horizontal, and the horizontal blocks the vertical. One ch'i smashes two, and two smash three. Let the opponent move smoothly, covering great distances, while I maintain my ease through sticking and connecting. If you ask from whence comes this marvelous secret, it is simply one movement of the ch'i.

Striking the Ch'i

It is like being startled in a dream, suddenly realizing the tao, experiencing an unexpected burning sensation on the skin, cold creeping up and causing a shiver, or suddenly thinking of a certain scene. The true ch'i, so turbulent and dense, is like thunder and lightning suddenly striking or smoke and flames from fire. Common students do not understand the "orifice of the primal source." Losing it, they seek elsewhere, but how could they thus gain enlightenment? When the muscles and skin are affected, they become unequaled in strength and hardness. Taking form, it penetrates deeply into the bones and marrow. Cutting through the construction (rong) and defense (wei) aspects of the body's energy levels, it arrives at the ch'i level. Whenever you touch the ch'i, there is pain; where there is pain, there is obstruction. All of this is perfectly logical. It blocks the path of the ch'i and blood and causes it to be interrupted; it stops the movement of the ch'i and blood and prevents it from circulating. It is possible to separate the bones, sever the tendons, and terminate life in a brief moment. How great indeed is the functioning of ch'i! One need only understand its accumulation, comprehend its projection, and master its application in order to entrap the opponent. To hit the bull's-eye with an arrow, you must adjust the body to eliminate leaning to either side, straighten your arrows and trim the feathers, and concentrate your central ch'i so that your spirit is focused and your ch'i full. If your drawing and releasing show perfect control of the square and round, then your determination to hit the target can shoot a poplar leaf [from a hundred paces] or pierce seven wooden writing tablets. It is all a matter of our skill in drawing back and releasing the arrow. The ch'i issues like the discharge of a cannon or a bolt from a crossbow, striking with a sudden impact. If you study these words, you will naturally achieve perfect accord between hand and mind. Do not take these words lightly.

It is precisely the same with the highest level of spirit. Wherever the spirit is focused, the ch'i will concentrate, and where the ch'i concentrates, the spirit also coalesces. When spirit and ch'i come together, form is born. Traces become attached to that which is connected with the form. The spirit and ch'i of life are active on this side, and the spirit and ch'i of death resonate on the other side. When the two aspects combine, they produce this form. Therefore, it is said: "The conditioned mind produces images," and also, "When there is perfect sincerity, metal and stone can be broken."

Enter After Finding an Opening

There is a saying that goes: liveliness takes advantage of an external opening; without finding an external opening, you will remain outside. In the martial arts, to overcome an opponent you must get in close, and then you will be able to throw them. Just like an object hidden in a room, without finding the door, you cannot enter. Even an expert could not do it. The arm has three openings: the wrists are the outer gate, the elbows are the middle gate, and the upper arm is the inner gate. When you have passed these three gates, you are already in the inner court and can then ascend to the hall and enter the room. Therefore, when one's approach to fighting is limited to just the hands and wrists, you will see bending and extending, back and forth, and fast and infinite changes. Fast hands prevail, while slow hands are defeated, but they can never decisively defeat an opponent and are themselves toppled with a single strike. If one fixes the mind on the elbow, although it is one level closer to the opponent's body, there are still opportunities for the opponent to neutralized our attack, and victory is not assured. The only way is to fix our concentration on the base of the opponent's upper arm, for then regardless of who strikes first, by paying attention to this point,

I am able to immobilize his hands and stick to him without losing contact. I can then change and act as I please with perfect ease, while my opponent will be unable to escape my control.

First Hand, Second Hand, and Front and Back Hands

When entering the outer gates and engaging in combat, there are ten errors that account for the failure to achieve victory. The first error is the inability to concentrate the ch'i prior to combat, being empty within, and issuing ch'i without speed or ferocity. The second error is the failure to position the hands below the chest in order to guard against attacks above and below. The third error is adopting a posture before engaging the opponent, which only serves to expose our weaknesses. The fourth error is advancing with an evasive posture and not daring to go straight ahead; this sacrifices the near in search of the distant and brings us toil without ease. The fifth error is advancing sidelong, changing postures, looseness, and inelegance. The sixth error is only making contact with the hands and wrists, not knowing how to close with the opponent. The seventh error is not following up after launching the first blow. The eighth error is holding the second hand tightly and still not striking. The ninth error is attacking decisively only after three or four attempts. The tenth error is dodging out of position and failing to stick. If you commit these ten errors, how can you avoid defeat? Accumulating ch'i and concentrating the spirit, positioning the hands below the chest, observing which foot the opponent advances and sticking to that side, focusing attention on the base of the opponent's upper arm, and controlling the upper arm are the method of breaching the opponent's defenses and dealing with all his actions. I strike first and then observe the root of his upper arm as he extends it. If my first hand is successful, I do not wait for the second. If he strikes first, I also observe the base of his upper arm, and then relax my attention, attack with force, and then slowly change. This method has the ingenuity of "opening an inch and separating a foot." Observing the root of the upper arm is "opening a inch," and then the hands "separate a foot." This is also the marvel of cutting off the ch'i and attacking the empty side. This is what is known as "surprising the opponent by attacking him where he is unprepared, like lightning that strikes before we can cover our ears." If I encounter fast hands that strike and withdraw chaotically, I do not change my hands or bend my arms, but smash the two ch'i and strike him. When I attack his left side, he will withdraw the left side and advance the right. I do not return the blow, but shifting, strike the root of his upper left arm. In this way, I am inside the circle, while he remains outside the circle. I am at ease, while he is greatly inconvenienced. No matter how smooth and fast the opponent, I invariably enjoy miraculous success. This is the secret of extending the forward hand and striking with the forward hand. Occasionally it is necessary to follow up with the rear hand, but this should be used appropriately and not forced. If used inappropriately, the motion will cause the body to turn sideways. This approach is an invitation to a strike and results from failing to understand this error.

The Head

The head is round like heaven. It is the meeting place of all the yang channels and the sea of the seminal essence and marrow. It is the locus of the connection between the governing and controlling vessels and the ruler of all the ch'i in the body. The entering and supporting of yin and yang both rely on the head. When this point is unified, then all the ch'i of the body enters; if it is not unified, then all the ch'i of the body is lost. It is essential to understand the specific locations where the ch'i is concentrated and focused. Forward bending postures allow the yang ch'i to enter. The head must incline forward and be lowered, and the ch'i sinks to the yin-t'ang point in the forehead between the eyebrows. Backward bending postures allow the yin ch'i to enter. The head must incline backward and be lifted, and the ch'i sinks to the Wind House point (feng fu, GV-16) just below the occiput at the back of the head. The entering of the ch'i occurs during both forward and sideways postures. When the head is inclined to the side, the ch'i sinks to the corner of the head above the ear. Diagonal and forward bending postures allow the diagonal entering of yin and yang. When the head is bent forward and cocked to the side, the ch'i sinks to the Sun and Moon points (ri yue, GB-24) at the corners of the forehead. In erect postures, where there is no leaning or inclining, and no bending forward or backward, yin and yang enter vertically. When the nose is straight ahead and vertical, the ch'i lands at the Hundred Convergences (bai hui, GV-20) at the center of the crown of the head. It is also important to understand that the method of encouraging the ch'i is to not drag or pull it. For example, when executing backward bending postures, the yin ch'i enters, the chin is raised, the chest is lifted up, the abdomen bulges, the hands are uplifted, and the toes are raised. In this way, the three points will be connected by one ch'i, and the yin ch'i will naturally enter. When executing forward bending postures, the yang ch'i enters, the chin is withdrawn, the back is curved, the hands are dropped, and the heels are raised. In this way, the three points are connected by one ch'i, and the yang ch'i naturally enters. When executing sideways postures, yin and yang both enter, the cheeks are lifted, the ribcage is raised, one foot is raised and the other is planted, one arm is raised and the other thrusts. In this way, the three points are connected by one ch'i, and yin and yang both enter. When executing vertically rising postures, yin and yang rush upward, the head pushes up, and the shoulders are raised. When the foot is lifted vertically, the knee should be raised; when it is not lifted vertically, the toes are lowered and the knee extended. In this way the three points are connected by one ch'i, and yin and yang both enter. Sideways, diagonal, bending forward, and bending backward can be similarly deduced.

The Feet

The ancients said that the head is round like heaven and the feet are square like earth. They also said that the hands are capable of both covering and turning over, and so resemble heaven, whereas the feet can cover but cannot turn over, and so resemble the earth. The feet are able to bear the weight of the entire body. In stillness, they are like mountains and possess the stability of huge stones; in movement, they are like oars, with no problem of leaning or inclining. They can be as still and unmoving, stable and unshakable as the earth. Its applications are divided into empty and full. The two feet, for example, may be divided into empty and full. In some cases the front foot is empty and the rear full, and in others the rear is empty and the front full. At other times, the left is empty and the right full, or the right empty and the left full. The foot itself includes toes, heel, edge, and sole, which may also be empty or full. In general, without fullness there is no stability, but absolute fullness restricts our freedom of movement, and one is easily toppled. Without emptiness there is no agility, but absolute emptiness causes lightness, floating, and instability, and one is easily shaken. When empty and full complement each other, one attains the marvel of naturalness. When the foot is extended and raised, or the toe is extended and enters below, then the ch'i descends and sinks. When the toes are raised and hook back, the ch'i ascends and floats. Foot positions may be described as crosswise and straight. These include both feet crosswise, both feet straight, and right angle stance, where one is crosswise and one is straight. There is obtuse angle stance, where the two feet are slightly turned out. There is goose stance, which is half crosswise and half straight. There is rotating and swinging. Rotating includes half turns, side tumbling cartwheels, and somersaults. Swinging includes swinging to the outside and swinging to the inside. There is sauntering and stepping. In sauntering, the foot extends backward; in stepping, the foot extends forward. There is treading and stamping. In treading, the foot tiptoes forward; in stamping, the foot cuts crosswise. There is twisting and pounding. In twisting, the toes are turned, and in pounding, the heel is planted. You must be able to mobilize the ch'i of the entire body. If when the body moves, the feet do not follow, there is dragging and pulling and the ch'i is scattered. How can we support the power of the front hand? The ch'i of the front hand is in the back foot. If the back foot does not follow, the ch'i of the body will not enter, one will be half restrained, and the ch'i will not be full. The feet are the boats of the body and the commanders of the legs. If there is the slightest disunity here, the ch'i of the entire body will fail to enter. The applications of foot techniques must be carefully analyzed. When springing forward in a sideways posture, the goose walking step is performed half diagonally and half straight ahead. When executing cross step and probing forward, or right angle step and slight forward horizontal, the rear leg is straight. When the body is inverted, upside down, and dragging, right angle step is also used. When the front foot is crosswise in back, the back foot is backwards straight. When executing four horizontals in a low posture, using obtuse angle stance with toes turned out, erect body thrusting upward, and double reverse stance with both feet rotated out, the backs of the feet and toes should be planted vertically. In vertical rising step, one foot is elevated and the other lowered. In forward advancing step, the rear foot moves first; in retreating step, the front foot moves first. When rising, the toes should be bent back; when sinking, the toes should be extended. In pressing forward with the body sideways, both feet are crosswise and pressed together. When the body advances straight forward, the front foot is slightly crosswise and the rear completely straight. Here the back foot moves first. When advancing forward with pressing step, the rear foot urges the front foot. In rushing step with slanted body, both feet are crosswise. In rushing step with the body straight ahead, the front foot is crosswise and the rear foot straight. In both cases the front foot moves first. When rushing forward and leading the back, the front foot brings along the back. When withdrawing the body sideways in retreat with the two feet both crosswise, or when withdrawing the body sideways in retreat with the front foot crosswise and the rear foot straight, the rear foot moves first, pulling back the front foot. When rising straight up and stepping crosswise, if you step left first move the right foot, and if you step right first move the left foot. In either case, raise the toes when rising, and extend the toes when sinking. When fighting wildly and without fixed steps, the toes of both feet are lifted however one pleases. In twisted step both rotating feet are reversed, and force is applied as we land on the outer edge of the foot. When I am pushed and retreat, the toes of both feet are lifted in reverse. When I am pushed but do not fall, I clutch and fall forward, arching the back and knocking the head against the ground, with both feet thrown in reverse. When retreating with stiff knees, cartwheel feet extend the toes and straighten the legs. You should not retreat with hooked feet. With calm ch'i in back and forth steps, the two feet pound fiercely, and I level the body and rush straight ahead. I have summarized the main elements in order to clarify the various permutations. In general, the secret is to let the steps follow the postures. Do not distort the postures or go against the ch'i: this is the secret of footwork.

The Hands

Wu Ch'eng said that the hands have five fingers, the fingers have three joints, and the thumb has one joint. Hidden within the thumb is the t'ai-chi symbol. Altogether there are fifteen joints, and both hands together equal thirty joints, representing the thirty days of one month. The days are shorter in the winter and longer in the summer, and equal in length during the spring and autumn. Therefore, the middle finger belongs to the heart; it rules summer, is the longest digit, and represents fire. The little finger belongs to the kidney; it rules winter, is the shortest digit, and represents water. The index finger belongs to the liver, and rules spring and wood. The ring finger belongs to the lungs, and rules autumn and metal. The index and ring fingers are equal in length, like the balance between spring and autumn. The thumb belongs to the spleen and rules earth. It flourishes in all four seasons and combines the four virtues. It is able to control one side all by itself. Therefore, if one or two of the fingers are missing, one can still grasp objects, but if the thumb is absent, the hand is useless. The marvel of bringing together the fingers is not borrowed or forced but completely natural. The finger techniques include "grinding hand," wherein the ch'i falls to the outer side of the little finger. In "swinging hand" the ch'i falls into the rear of the palm. In these two hand techniques, the five fingers are all lined up in order, and the fingertips are turned over and lifted. In the remaining hand techniques the fingers should be curled back, arranged in a circle, and with the joints hooked tightly like a bow. In this way, the ch'i is raised and concentrated without scattering.

For example, in "vertical opponent's hand" and "returning hook hand" the thumb and little finger work in opposition and lead the ch'i. Water must unite with earth. The one of heaven gives birth to water, which together with the five of earth equals six. In horizontal yin hand and horizontal yang hand, the thumb and middle finger work in opposition and lead the ch'i. Fire must unite with earth. The two of earth gives birth to fire, which together with the five of heaven equals seven. In "upturned welcoming hand," the thumb and index finger work in opposition and lead the ch'i. Wood must unite with earth. The three of heaven gives birth to water, and together with the five of earth, equals eight. In "yin ward-off hand," the thumb and ring finger work in opposition and lead the ch'i. Metal must unite with earth. The four of earth gives birth to metal, which together with the five of heaven equals nine. Thus it can be seen that metal, wood, water, and fire cannot possibly be without earth. It is thus understood that there is a fixed and unchanging law to the combining of fingers. If there is the slightest error, the ch'i does not enter. When it comes to applications, there are nine principles: 1) straight forward and straight back, 2) turn palm up, scoop, and carry, 3) turn palm down, sink, and lower, 4) hook out and swing out, 5) hook in and embrace, 6) diagonal scooping to the upper right, 7) diagonal splitting to the lower left, 8) diagonal leading to the upper left, and 9) diagonal pulling to the lower right. The four sides and four corners, together with the straight projection of the middle path, correspond to the nine palaces.

The Fist

The fist is flexed and not extended, and the fingers are grasped firmly so as to concentrate the ch'i. The method of clenching the fist is to pinch the crease of the third joint of the index finger with the tip of the thumb. The four fingers are clenched tightly and exert force in unison. By remaining inseparable, they do not scatter when attacking, and thus benefit from the secret of unity. In this way, earth permeates the four virtues and is the method of unifying the five phases. The applications involve the four sides and four corners, and combining these with the central palace, produce the nine methods. The ch'i does not seize upon the entire body, and the landing place must have a definite location. Learn from each situation and do not apply techniques in a confused manner. For example, when horizontal yin hand strikes downward, the second joint of the middle finger leads the ch'i; when horizontal yang hand thrusts upward, the knuckle of the middle finger leads the ch'i. When a sideways fist thrusts upward, the second joint of the thumb leads the ch'i; when a sideways fist chops downward, the knuckle of the little finger leads the ch'i. When striking straight ahead without regard for horizontal or sideways, the area between the knuckle and second joint of the little finger leads the ch'i.

Preface on the Origins of the Martial Arts

The martial arts were not created by divine beings, but by ordinary people. In less than three weeks and in one's spare time one can practice sideways and straight ahead, bending forward and bending backward, high and low, extended and contracted, horizontal stepping and disorderly reversal, advance and retreat, and stepping and treading. These postures are often brought forth, but it is a pity that they cannot be strung together. I followed my teacher for over forty years, and through repeated investigations, have gained some slight understanding and dispelled a mass of misapprehensions. I then realized the truth of the words, "If you seek with sincerity, you will find more than enough teachers." I now have many students of my own and therefore have written this in clear language to facilitate their study. I will elaborate on the boxing methods below.

The Twenty-Four Postures of Combined Training

The method of combined training is the fifth level of training the body, wherein the body and ch'i are unified. It is the method for completing one's training. It includes rising and falling, high and low, sideways and straight, bending forward and bending backward, diagonal and twisting, all of which have specific techniques. Altogether there are seventy-two postures that correspond to the seventy-two stages of development. Multiplying the postures, we derive 360 that correspond to the 365 degrees. 360 is too complex and difficult to practice, but condensing these to the essentials, there are seventy-two. Further dividing these into three parts, we have high, middle, and low, with twenty-four postures in each, that correspond to the twenty-four climatic ch'i. The high twenty-four postures include rising vertically, flying, and dancing; the lower twenty-four postures include coiling on the ground, rolling, and lying prostrate; the middle twenty-four postures are neither vertical rising nor coiling on the ground, but middle horizontal postures. Human beings are endowed with the ch'i of heaven and earth, yin and yang. The ascending and descending proceed from high to low. The arrangement of the three powers [heaven, man, and earth] is a natural principle. However, vertical rising and coiling on the ground should not be practiced too quickly by beginners. Therefore, although these middle twenty-four postures do not exhaust all the permutations of the middle level, nevertheless they are a good starting point for beginners. When you have practiced them until they feel easy, and every posture is perfected, then go on to master the forty-eight high and low postures. All possible variations can then be multiplied infinitely. Why bother to memorize many forms, that wear us out for years and years? Prior to this, one should separately train the legs, arms, hands, feet, head, shoulders, elbows, body, internal ch'i, attracting ch'i, and source ch'i. When it comes to unifying the head, hands, and feet, developing continuity between postures, and balancing hard and soft, without precision and practice the three points will not be accurate and landing will not be solid. If the three points are not coordinated, timing is poor, and yin and yang are in disorder, the ch'i will not flow, hard and soft will be turned upside down, and there will be pulling above and dragging below. In this state it is impossible to expect the stability of Mount Tai and the agility of a crafty hare. The body contains ch'i, and ch'i propels the body. When the body is unified, the ch'i flows, and when the ch'i flows, the body is naturally agile. Without these two conditions, it is useless to seek elsewhere for help. The training method for achieving this is to master all the postures, and then the three points will be coordinated. When we have perfected movement and stillness, the three points will be unified. Yin will transform into yang, and yang into yin; you cannot break continuity and keep starting over. Move the ch'i with softness and land with hardness. The two must complement each other and follow in the proper sequence. If the ch'i from above is below, or the ch'i from below is above, then you will need to correct the pulling and dragging; if the ch'i from the front is in back, or the ch'i from the back is in front, then you will need to free the obstructions. If your postures have not coordinated the three points, your landing will not be successful. Only with the three points is landing possible. Without the three mobilizations [mind, ch'i, and spirit], the ch'i will not arrive, and if they do not arrive, do not attempt to strike. In killing postures, analyze the transformations; in saving postures, pay attention to every detail. If you practice in this way, you will find that training produces mastery. By not violating principles, your skill will become marvelous and will never leave you. Those who only train the external body and do not understand this higher level of practice have everything backward when it comes to applications; they use lots of force but gain little success. How can they be unaware that to get to the bottom of this art they must acknowledge that inner alchemy is the secret of heaven and earth. These secrets are only transmitted to the right person at the right time and at the right place. Those who receive my teachings, can on the highest level become enlightened and transcend the mortal realm, and at very least strengthen their bodies, eliminate illness, and achieve longevity. It is not simply a matter of hardness overcoming sharpness and calling this mastery of the art. All of my students must be extremely careful; they must treasure these teachings and not recklessly reveal them to unworthy men. Otherwise they will be punished by heaven and suffer bitterness in their hearts.

Train the body so that it unites with the ch'i; train the ch'i so that it reverts to spirit; and train the spirit so that it returns to the void. The body consists of hands, feet, organs, and bones; the ch'i is the circulation of yin and yang; the spirit is the subtle essence of the mind, which responds immediately to contact and senses and communicates with the environment; the void is infinity. Yin and yang are based on t'ai-chi, and t'ai-chi is based on infinity. The void at its highest contains heaven and earth; the void at its highest contains the fullness of heaven and earth. It is without visible image, cannot be captured, and leaves no trace. Only by using no force can we bring out natural force, which changes easily and does not impede us.

Allow me to explain the condition that precedes the twenty-four characters. The twenty-four characters associated with the twenty-four postures are all aspects of a single word: ch'i. Every posture must be executed with ch'i, which is involved in all twenty-four characters. It is just that it expresses itself differently in responding to different situations. All twenty-four postures represent the method of absorbing ch'i. Let us explain the relationship between absorbing ch'i and the head and face. The head is the first site of absorbing ch'i. The main practice is to trace four circles: circle left and around to the right; circle right and around to the left; circle to the front and around to the back; circle to the back and around to the front. While doing this, crease the brow and contract the nose. Withdraw the upper lip and extend the lower lip as if to curl the nose. This is what is called, "absorbing ch'i is like swallowing a stream," meaning that it is as if the mouth was swallowing something. By inhaling with all your might, you will fully absorb the ch'i. The front, back, left, and right circles naturally follow the postures. There is one posture for each circle, not four circles for each posture.

Cultivating the Ch'i

Ch'i connects with the nine heavens above and the nine springs below; it spans the nine continents in the middle. It exists and permeates everywhere. It is compressed in the heart and fills the whole body. To express it effectively you must know the secrets. Although the six bowels govern the ch'i, it is most fully expressed in the five viscera; although the ch'i is gathered together in the five viscera, it exits through the six bowels. Where are the six bowels located? They are located above. Where are the five viscera located? They are located below. What is located in the middle of the above and below? It is called the Yellow Chamber, Gate of the Source, T'ai-chi Chamber, or Pivot of the Tao. What fills above is the Gate of Heaven; what culminates below is the Earth Axis. The Moon Cave issues from the Gate of Heaven, and the Heavenly Root comes forth from the Earth Axis. Circulating amidst the thirty-six palaces between the Gate of Heaven and the Moon Cave is spring, the source of c'hi. Just like flowing water, with each inhalation it courses a thousand miles, and with each exhalation a thousand miles. The secret lies in fully exercising the mind, which is where the ch'i collects. When it enters the Spirit Chamber, it becomes as hard as the golden elixir. Its roundness is like a rolling pearl; its squareness is like a carpenter's square. Its expression in the head manifests as the five phases; its functioning in the body manifests as yin and yang. The five phases must follow the interaction of yin and yang, and when yin and yang proceed from one unified ch'i, it becomes so supremely great and strong that nothing can contain it. This is what is meant by, "The tao permeates heaven and earth and transcends form."

In this book, what we mean by training the c'hi refers to external methods; internal training is found in the *Yi-chin ching* (Sinew changing classic). Beginners should not attempt to train the ch'i, but should first develop body techniques and footwork. You must not use strength, but following each posture naturally, slowly perform them in a dance-like way. Devote yourself to harmonizing the body into a unified whole. Next make your movements light, lively, rounded, and well-practiced. If your body mechanics are awkward, regulate your opening and closely appropriately for each posture. As you execute each posture make sure that all the sinews and bones are relaxed and open. Practice this a hundred times each day.

Above is the trigram *Li* (The Clinging) and below is the trigram *Kan* (The Abysmal). *Li* is empty in the middle and at the crown of the head represents yin; *Kan* is full in the middle and at the ming-men point between the kidneys represents yang. The Central Palace is located just below the umbilicus and is the Yellow Chamber. This is where yin and yang interact. The heart is the sovereign fire, and the ming-men is the ministerial fire. When the sovereign fire stirs, the ministerial fire follows it. The sovereign fire is the ruler, and the ministerial fire supports it. The fire is the ch'i of the liver and is yang. The yang ch'i in the Palace of K'an travels from the back to the front, and rises from below to above. The yin ch'i of the Palace of Li descends from above to below. The two ch'i interact in the Central Palace. In this way, the ch'i accumulates, and when the ch'i accumulates, power is born.

Secret Transmission of Training the Ch'i

The mind is the essence of the ch'i,
And the ch'i is the function of the mind.
The five phases are rooted in one mind,
And yin and yang are in balance.
Although the whole body is unified top to bottom,
There are local distinctions,
Such that the front may be yang and the rear yin,
Or leaning backward may be light and bending forward
    heavy.
When yin returns to a yin site, there is binding;
When yang returns to a yang site, there is movement.
Above is the starting point of yin;
Below is the fulfillment of yang.
Above and below coalesce in the center.
The central ch'i is exceedingly strong:

Above it rushes up to heaven;
Below it provides the stability of mountains.
It returns to the left and revolves to the right;
Returns to the right and pulls to the left.
It advances forward like flowing water,
And strikes upward like raising a mountain.
It lands like a flying stone,
And issues forth as from a bowstring.
Ch'i issues forth with the sound of the wind,
And is absorbed like swallowing a stream.
It runs ahead like stars chasing the moon,
And retreats like a rolling raspberry.
The fingers are hooked together in application;
The shoulders are like wielding tongs.
Above and below are one unified ch'i;
When the people are prosperous the nation is naturally at
    peace.
Knowing this secret transmission,
Your practice will not be difficult.

The advancing, retreating, movement, and stillness of one body are all controlled by the mind. The mind is the ruler and issues orders. The mind being formless is able to give form to form and remain formless in its midst. The power of reflection brings knowledge, and the Life Gate (ming-men, GV-4) supports it. The Life Gate is the birthplace of the ch'i and the axis of the whole body. It plays the role of minister and transmits the orders of the ruler. The head leads the hands and feet. The head supervises the various assistants and is the commander-in-chief, sending the great ministers about their duties. The hands and feet play the role of underlings. Therefore, the movements in each posture originate in the mind; the ming-men is next, then the head, and finally the hands and feet. When the spirit moves, heaven follows; let everything be natural. Any affectations will lead to failure. Operations are in the hands, but transformations follow the mind in response to the situation. Sheer force will not carry the day.

Absorbing Ch'i

When you hold the head up high, the ch'i of the throat easily enters. You should slightly draw in the upper lip and thrust the lower lip forward like an elephant curling its nose. The two channels beginning at the corners of the eyes contract all the way to the corners of the mouth. The channel running up the spine rises from the waist, and passing over the crown of the head, finally reaches the upper lip. Now rising from the heart along the front of the body, it arrives at the lower lip. Absorbing ch'i involves four circles. The first circle is from left to right; the second circle is from right to left; the third circle is from below to above; the fourth circle is from above to below. This applies to the head and is used in leaning postures.

The Central Ch'i

The ch'i issues from the kidneys, moving from the back to the front and passing through the crotch, then from below surging straight up. You must seal the anus to prevent the ch'i from draining downward. When the ch'i surges up to the chest, it seeks to escape. At this time you must inhale forcefully with the mouth and seal the throat. The ch'i will move straight from above to below, ultimately reaching the tan-t'ien. When the shoulders hang, the elbows sink, and the flanks are constrained, then the ch'i is raised to the Central Palace and does not extend to the chest. Inhaling the ch'i is what is meant by absorbing the ch'i as if swallowing a stream. The ch'i must travel up and down within the body. If you only have an intellectual understanding and not a real grasp, this is false and inauthentic. It is not only useless, but may actually be harmful to your health.

The External Body

The head is the commander of the body. The body orders the arms, and the arms order the fingers. The ming-men is the pivot of the entire body. The head is like a dragonfly lightly touching the water; the fists are like butting rams. The waist is like a crowing cock who curls his tail. Because it is curled, the ch'i moves from back to front, gathers and is not scattered. The feet are like purple swallows entering the forest. The crotch is open in front and closed behind. The center is round. The Hundred Convergences point is located at the crown of the head, and the Gushing Spring is located in the ball of the foot. The Meeting of Yin point (hui yin, CV-1) is located at the perineum. The ch'i of the Hundred Convergences sinks downward, and the ch'i of the Gushing Spring rises upward. The ch'i of the Meeting of Yin supports the whole body. The ch'i of above and below gathers together in the Central Palace and is unified.

Great and Small Postures

In closing postures do not mind its smallness; in opening postures do not mind its greatness. If you want to issue power, it is not just a matter of expanding the body to make it great or contracting it to make it small.

Power is natural power, and so at the beginning of training it is imperative that we not use strength.

Practicing the Art

When assuming a posture, the ch'i should be relaxed and lively. The ch'i supports but is not hard. When it lands on the opponent, exert all your power. By expressing the power of your entire life, you will realize the marvel of the complementary relationship of hard and soft.

Note on "exerting power": After completing a cycle, exert all the power of your flesh and bones on one point. The power is exerted internally, but appears to be external. All the ch'i of the entire body must be raised. The center of the crown of the head should be lifted up before assuming any posture. The weight of the body should be distributed precisely in the middle of the two legs, so that in rising straight up or sinking straight down one will not commit the error of constant imbalance.

The foot should not be placed flat. When the whole foot makes contact with the ground, and one exerts maximum effort, the result will be an inhibition of free movement. Only by using the toes to make contact with the ground will one be free of instability and grossness when landing a blow.

The most important thing is that the three points be coordinated. The three points are the head, hands, and feet. The second requirement is that the ch'i mobilize the "three exertions." The "exertions" are horns. The head, hands, and feet are the three horns.

When practicing the art, the arms must be soft and lively, and no strength should be used. The fists should be clenched tightly and held level with the arms. They must not be bent back, hooked down, or everted to the outside. The arms should be soft and lively as they move in and out, and only then can one achieve speed and ferocity and not fall into hardness, stiffness, or inhibition. When the fist is tightly clenched and held level with the arms, one can achieve the proper sinew method. When sticking to the opponent's skin, the whole body is like a thunderbolt. The moment that hostility arises, the three points all fall into place. Only in this way can we strike with power, and make it difficult for our opponent to respond. If the fist is tilted back in an attitude similar to lifting the head, hooked down in the shape of a hook, or deviated as if twisting the crown, then not only will we be weak, but our blows will have no weight and we will simply injure our own hands and arms. In gathering the joints, the forward joints are gathered to the rear, and the rear joints are gathered to the front. The upper joints are gathered to the lower, and the lower joints are gathered to the upper. This is what is meant when it is said that in unity there is no place that is not unified.

On the subject of cycling, half of complete unity is a small cycle. Martial arts postures include direct attacks, or issuing postures, and circling postures, where the hand twists. This is what we mean by cycling and may be summed up in the one phrase "retreat becomes advance." However, bear in mind that unity must precede the unity of the hands. First rouse your own ch'i power, gathering it together in a cycle. Then when you engage in combat, because you take the initiative, your postures may not yet stick to the opponent's body, and therefore you should not issue strength from your upper body. In this way, you must cycle in order to raise the opponent's ch'i. If you have already closed with the opponent, then when you assume a posture, you may find that you are still deficient. Therefore, it is necessary to exert yourself, and only then will the ch'i force emerge and be unstoppable. As a result, students of this art must first practice large circles and then gradually small circles. At the level of perfect mastery, the circles become invisible and are known only by the mind, leaving no trace.

Borrowing Ch'i

"Borrowing ch'i" refers to borrowing the opponent's ch'i to strike the opponent. When the opponent's strike is just about to land on our body, we take advantage of this to make our move. This leaves the opponent no opportunity to retreat or to block. There is no more marvelous principle. If we make our move prematurely, this allows the opponent time to retreat; if we make our move too late, then we have already been beaten. This is the principle of "strike second but land first." In this way, seize opportunities and go into action. If you act at the right time, you need never worry about your lack of skill. This is what is meant by turning an opponent's scheme against him and borrowing strength to apply strength. This is also what is meant by striking the enemy when they are in disarray.

Seizing the Ch'i

I have heard that in engaging in combat it is possible to first seize the opponent's ch'i. Blocking the opponent's hand is called the first gate; blocking their elbow is called the second gate; and controlling their shoulder is called the third gate. Therefore, when engaging the opponent, you must first control the shoulder. This is the highest level of mastery. Seek it and seize it, and the opponent will automatically be unable to move his hands, while I enjoy freedom of movement.

The classics state: "Attack where the enemy is unprepared and take him by surprise."[5] They also state: "His power is awesome and his attack focused."[6] And also: "If you value miraculous swiftness, wait in comfort for your opponent's discomfort."[7] You must understand these ideas well.

There is no mystery to the method for achieving freedom of movement. It is born of practice and realized in stillness.

When it comes to exertion, as you are about to land a blow and worry that your strength is insufficient and your ch'i lacking, then gather your bones and flesh and bring them to bear on one point, exerting your strength to the maximum. This is like a fowling piece that is loaded with powder. Now use a ramrod to compress the powder until it is very firm. At this point, if a spark is introduced power will be released. This is why we speak of circling back. Other works speak of lightning-like speed that follows exertion. Without the word "exertion" we cannot begin to understand this kind of power.

The Unity of Three Ch'i Into One

In assuming our first posture, even before closing with the opponent, you must concentrate your ch'i. When the ch'i is concentrated, the sovereign fire [heart] stirs and the ministerial fire [ming men] supports it. It begins in the lower back and is gathered in the front. The yang ch'i rushes upward to the chest and diaphragm and is then absorbed in the mouth. From the lungs it then descends. The sinking yin ch'i enters the tan-t'ien where yin and yang interact. This is what is meant by the liver ch'i rising and the lung ch'i sinking, or the unity of the two forces. The ch'i of the whole body advances forward, and the ch'i below again surges upward. Once again the mouth absorbs ch'i, drawing it to a point above the umbilicus and below the heart. When the upper body sinks down, all the joints of the body are bound together. Make them strong and firm. Although the body advances fiercely, the arms and hands should be held back. This is called "circling back." Circling back is half unity. In this way, the posture advances, but the ch'i becomes increasingly concentrated. As the whole body rushes forward, the hands circle back. The joints naturally draw tightly together and become harder than steel and stone. These are the two ch'i. When you are about to land a blow, if you are still worried that your strength is insufficient and you have no opportunity to circle back, then draw the bones and flesh together in one place. This is called exertion and may be referred to as the third ch'i. This is like an explosive. The more tightly it is wrapped, the more forcefully it resounds. Thus first learn concentration, next circling back, and finally exertion. When your skill matures, the three ch'i unite in one and become useful. In closing, everything closes; in opening, everything opens. Above is yang, and below is yin. Stillness is yin, and movement is yang. Retreat is yin, and advance is yang. The ch'i surging upward is yang; absorbing downward is yin. The back is yang, and the belly is yin. Extending the hands is yang; withdrawing the hands is yin. We cannot limit our discussion to just one aspect. Turning up is yang; covering is yin. In softness we move the ch'i; in hardness we land our blows.

Achieving Equilibrium and Raising

When heaven and earth interact, the ten thousand things are born. When we neither lean nor incline, the ch'i reaches equilibrium. For a thousand autumns and ten thousand years, we constantly raise and concentrate. Only with harmony and unity is the one ch'i pervasive.

The Liver Rises and the Lung Descends

Endings and beginnings, ten thousand things, spring and
    autumn;
Yin and yang, rising and falling, one ch'i circulates everywhere.
If you want to understand liver rising and lung descending,
Just look at the inhalation and exhalation of the breath.

The liver belongs to wood and therefore it produces fire. When the liver fire stirs, the ch'i from below rises up. This is yang. The ch'i is what gives rise to strength, and the source of ch'i is the Life Gate and Central Pole (zhong ji, CV-3). Therefore, the yang ch'i is below and the lungs belong to metal. Metal restrains wood, therefore it is able to control the liver ch'i and cause it to descend. The descending is yin, therefore we say that the yin ch'i is above. The ch'i below issues forth and is inexhaustible. The yang ch'i rises up. The ch'i above is absorbed and sealed and not allowed to escape. The yin ch'i descends, and the two ch'i interact in the Central Palace. Therefore, we call it the central ch'i.

The Old and Young Follow Each Other

The young follows the old, and the old follows the young.
When the old and young follow each other marvels natu-
    rally appear;
When there is perfect accord, issue in unison.
Why fear the opponent's timing and skill?

The Conversion and Combining of Yin and Yang

Yin becomes yang and yang becomes yin.
Yin and yang convert and combine, but share a common
    root.
If you want to understand the principle of the conversion
    and combining of yin and yang,
Then seek it in the place where yin and yang mutually
    convert.

The Source of Courage Ch'i

The right ch'i of heaven and earth comes together in my
    body.

When it is abundant, it fills the whole body everywhere.
This is what Mencius meant by "vast."
What other ch'i could compare with it?

The Functioning of the Five Phases

The liver plays host, occupying the trigram *Chen* (The
   Arousing) in the east.
The spleen rules in the central palace.
The heart governs the fire of the trigram *Li* (The Clinging)
   and spiritual transformations.
When the kidney function is flourishing, the ch'i strength is
   full.
If you want to know the duties of the lung,
It is dispersion and control.
This is the marvelous functioning of the five phases.
If you breathe properly, you will naturally reach perfection.

Song of the Central Ch'i

Never say that the "baby boy" and "beautiful maiden" can
   separate.
In the middle is the "yellow matchmaker," who catalyzes
   the miraculous marriage.[8]
Reversal and intercourse take place in the "yellow chamber."
The bride and groom tremble, embrace, and fall in love.

The Head

The head is like heaven and belongs to the trigram *Ch'ien*
   (The Creative).
Sideways and front, bending backward and forward are all
   natural.
The minor yin and minor yang both arise from this.
Yin and yang, entering and attaching are no trifling matters.

The Groin

One side of the groin rises and the other sinks.
The uses of rising and sinking, high and low are many.
The pivot of the lower body is precisely here.
This is an area you must not neglect.

The Hand

The shoulders hang and the ten fingers connect.
The cycle of engendering and restraining is completed by
    the five phases.
The opponent receives a horizontal push, watching the
    three extremes.
Penetrate straight ahead: these are the three transmissions.

The Feet

The feet tread the earth in a posture like mountains.
Touching, reversing, and stepping flat naturally.
When freely jumping and touching down,
Raise the ch'i, and make contact with the toes.

The Elbows

The two hands hang, and the elbows bend.
Three invitations of Chu-ko Liang put the opponent in
    jeopardy.
From bent to straight, and from straight back to bent,
It seems that close applications are superior to distant.

The Knees

The elbows have sharp angles, and the knees have caps.
The knee caps are even mightier than the elbows,

Hooking and connecting to the left and right, and then
   quickly kneeling.
Golden Cock Stands on One Leg is a technique most
   difficult to withstand.

Level Shoulders

Both shoulders are raised as if carrying a burden.
The rising ch'i is concentrated at the points of the shoulders.
The opening of the chest and closing of the back is a
   natural wonder.
When the twin peaks match, we have an air of dignity.

Tilted Shoulders

One shoulder is high and the other is low.
High and low, eschewing evenness.
Low and elevated alternate with countless transformations.
Seven strokes and ten postures with many surprises.

On the Subject of Action

Express spirit on the inside;
Express ease on the outside.
He looks like a maiden,
But explodes like a tiger.
One of my disciples
Is equal to a hundred opponents.

On the Subject of Fighting

Whether your postures are sideways or straight, the body should
be squarely in the middle of the two legs. The three points should be
coordinated so that there is no early and late.
   The legs should not be too widely separated, and the hands should

not be overextended. If the legs are too wide, the body cannot easily rotate, and it will be difficult to avoid being thrown. If you overextend the hands, your turns will not be subtle, and your lower postures will not manifest.

Fighting is like the military formation called "Mount Ch'ang snake." If you attack its head, the tail responds; if you attack its tail, the head responds; and if you attack its center, both head and tail respond.

On the Subject of Pressure Points

Before the ch'i moves, the mind moves first.
Once the mind moves, the ch'i charges.
The movement of the mind is like a cannon or fire.
The ch'i arrives like a bolt from a crossbow.
If students can marshal their primal ch'i,
What need have they to fear an opponent's superior skill?

Never say that pressure points are just isolated spots,
For the entire spirit must be mobilized.
This is like being startled in a dream,
Like sudden enlightenment to the tao,
Like a hot flash on the skin,
Like a sudden shiver or shudder,
Or lightning issuing from thick clouds.
As fast as a shudder,
Just think of the scene,
And the fierceness is there.

On Striking

When I strike straight ahead, the opponent wards off,
	seizes my arm, and attempts to throw me.
Ward-off inserts, throw is accompanied by a stamp, and
	seizing raises up.

Hard and soft complement each other like a turning wheel,
Or just like a sudden burning flash.

On Blocking

When the opponent strikes to the left, I strike to the right.
Why seek forever in the same place?
When the vertical comes, I block horizontally with the
    ferocity of lightning.
I take advantage of the opponent's sinking to throw him
    down.

On the Hands and Feet

When extending the hands, drop the shoulders and bring
    the elbows together.
Support to the left and right like flowing water.
When attacked, head and tail work together as if connected
    by a single thread.
In our fighting technique, why bother with ward-off, seize,
    and hook?

Fast Techniques

Looser and looser, relaxed and more relaxed.
Before my ch'i stirs, I seem like a sick old man.
Suddenly a spring lightning bolt strikes,
And a thousand chariots and ten thousand horses charge
    across the battlefield.

Rising Up Forcefully

The technique lies in exhaling the pure and reversing the foul,
And especially in cultivating stillness.

The Secret Transmission of Fighting

If the opponent does not move, I do not move;
When the opponent is about to move, I move first.

How To Begin Study

In general, at the beginning of study it is important to relax and enliven the shoulders, so that they are not stiff and hard. The elbows should be connected with the body and sink downward to form a horizontal circle. The toes should remain in contact with the ground, and the foot should not be planted flat. If the foot is flat, lifting the feet will be inhibited. The front foot should step directly forward, with the toes touching the ground, and the rear foot at an angle. However, the foot should not be too full, causing the whole foot to be planted. The head should follow the postures, so that the head is in yang position with yang postures and yin position with yin postures. When the posture is neither yin nor yang, the head too is neither yin nor yang. In unbalanced or twisted postures, the head too is unbalanced and twisted. The hands, as they move to the left and right, bending and extending, should follow the opponent as he moves in an out. There is no fixed pattern. My hands bend and extend, move high and low, following the opponent as he moves in and out, high and low. However, there is a definite pattern to the bending and extending of the legs. The front leg should not be too bent. If it is too bent, we commit the error of kneeling. At the same time, it should not be too straight. If it is too straight, we are guilty of stiffness. The bending or extension of the rear leg depends completely on the size of our footwork. When we take large steps, the legs should be open and relaxed, so that the power can be expressed. When we take small steps, the rear leg bends and extends in approximate correspondence with the bending and extension of the front leg. The forward and backward bending of the body also depends completely on the size of our footwork. With large steps, the body is inclined slightly forward in half sideways posture; with small steps, the body should be placed between the two feet, also in half sideways posture. The three points should be coordinated, so that the nose, hands, and feet form a single line connecting above and below. The three points all arrive together, such that the eyes, fists, and feet all arrive together, with no earlier and later. The three unities are feet, hands, and eyes. Any time you are prepared to strike, you must weigh what posture to adopt and where to strike. Our visual focus, our target, and the direction of the toes must all advance together. No matter what offensive posture you adopt, if you want to strike with power and firmness, the front foot should not be limited to either the inside or outside of the opponent's feet. Your toes should seek to seize the ground behind the opponent. When the three points are coordinated, all will be well. When it comes to opening the opponent's door, regardless of left or right, the hard bony part of my wrist inserts itself above the soft fleshy part of the arm in front of the elbow and powerfully splits it like cutting firewood with an axe. Once you have split the opponent's arms, you can then follow this up and land your blow. In this way, my postures will be successful, and the opponent will not be able to slip away. The head is like a dragonfly skimming the water; the fists are like a ram's butting horns; and the feet are like swallows entering the woods. The principle of landing a strike is like lightning flashing in the clouds. We issue energy like a bolt shooting from a crossbow. If students apply themselves conscientiously, they can reach the realm of great subtlety.

At the beginning of study do not speak of training the ch'i, but first develop your body, footwork, and eye techniques. It is also important not to use strength, but rather execute each posture naturally and slowly in circular dance-like movements. Coordinate the whole body into a unified whole, and then cause it to be light, lively, and perfect. Wherever there is stiffness and awkwardness release these one by one according to the postures. As you perform each posture, relax and open all the joints in the body. In this way, you will reach a marvelous level.

Points to Keep in Mind for Beginners

Study in a quiet place and do not show off or talk boastfully about your art. Only then will you reach the highest level. The *Analects* says: "Artisans occupy their shops and carry out their work. Gentlemen study in order to develop their tao." Surely this is the truth.

Take your martial arts study seriously and do not consider it child's play. In this way, you will avoid falseness and carelessness.

In studying martial arts, you must understand the principles and communicate the spirit. Pay attention to the names of the postures and reflect on their form. In this way, you will realize the finer points.

No matter whether the postures are inclined, straight ahead, reversed, or sideways, the body should be centered between the two legs. In this way, you will be as unshakable as Mount Tai. If there is the slightest imbalance, there will be twisting to the east and splitting to the west, toppling to the south and faltering to the north. How can you avoid falling and being a laughing stock?

In practicing martial arts, the front foot should be planted crosswise with the ch'i of the center of the big toe hooked toward the inside, and the rear foot planted firmly with the heel twisted outward. The two knees face each other, so that not only is there no chance of instability, but the crotch is also protected.

Footwork should not be too wide, lest if you panic and are at a loss, you will not topple and fall. By not worrying about wide stances, you will be able to jump high. The word "high" is more important than the word "far." This will serve you well.

In studying martial arts, when the left moves, the right responds.

When the right attacks, the left supports it. When left and right generate each other, we experience the marvel of yin and yang circulating throughout the body.

In studying martial arts, we should invest all of our strength, for only then can we become powerful. This is like the lion who uses all of his strength to attack an elephant and also uses all of his strength to attack a rabbit. In this way, our whole spirit is fully expressed, and there is no obstacle we cannot overcome. If one complains of a lack of strength, is the problem not with oneself?

Wherever stiffness exists, we should sink as we express power; turning points in the body should be lively and sensitive.

In studying martial arts, you should express your power and preserve your ch'i. In expressing power, every part of the body is mobilized for battle; in preserving the ch'i, you should raise it every step of the way. Within raising there is battle; within battle there is raising. Emerging, submerging, and transforming, we should not simply imitate things. If we imitate things, we will be in error.

In studying martial arts, the feet and hands should be coordinated; the hands and eyes should be coordinated; the eyes and mind should be coordinated; the mind and spirit are coordinated; the spirit and ch'i are coordinated; and the ch'i and body are coordinated. There is no other secret to skill and harmony.

In studying martial arts, the most important thing is practice. The blood and ch'i of the whole body must circulate freely, and then it will be filled with one unified ch'i.

In studying the martial arts, the first priority is character. In all things the practitioner should be respectful and humble. The true gentleman is not contentious.

To perfect a given posture takes approximately a thousand repetitions. If it is not yet perfected, you need another thousand repetitions.

Students of martial arts should be very reserved. Every movement should express calmness and harmony. Welcome everyone with friendliness and greet disaster with equanimity.

Do not attempt to share your interest in martial arts with pedantic, narrow-minded scholars. As soon as they find out, they will quote from the classics and regale you will all kinds of irrelevant nonsense. This is infuriating. You can deal with this either by avoiding them or by keeping your art private.

Do not casually test your art with violent ruffians. If you are lucky, they will simply dismiss you; if you are not so lucky, they will become angry and hostile. When you spy these types, be very deferential and do not insult them. In this way, they will be satisfied and even happy to support you.

Do not lightly reveal or transmit your art to others. If you lightly reveal it, they will simply regard it as idle talk and will not take it seriously; if you lightly transmit it, then criminals will become involved, and you will be implicated.

At the beginning of study, you should first put your body techniques in order and attend to your footwork and eyes. You should not say that you will first get the general idea and then correct the details. If you approach it this way, you will never get it right. The *I ching* says: "To receive teachings and cultivate them correctly is the work of sagehood."

Students of the martial arts must be righteous and not use their art to commit criminal acts, discredit their conduct and character, and shame themselves and forfeit their lives. The *Yin-fu ching* says:

"When the true gentleman finds the secret, he becomes righteous; when the petty man finds the secret, he forfeits his life." Pay attention to this.

The martial artist should be upright, sober, and reserved. You should take being a righteous hero as your mission and sagehood as your method. Only then can you achieve wisdom and preserve your body.

Students of the martial arts should strive for understanding of the mind and spirit, for broad learning and worldliness. What others are ignorant of, you should know; what others are incapable of doing, you should be able to do. Examining the tip, you grasp the whole; hearing one sound, you know everything. In this way, you can be a master.

To study martial arts you must be single-minded and ambitious, devoted and hard-working. In this way, you will make progress every day. If your practice is superficial, and if you are merely showing off and mistakenly believe that you are highly accomplished, you will simply embarrass yourself. Confucius said: "His character was such that he was enthusiastic to the point of forgetting to eat, joyful to the point of forgetting suffering, and was oblivious to the approach of old age." How profound this is!

In studying the martial arts, first look at the twenty-four orthodox postures and then look at the set of unorthodox postures. The orthodox are for establishing the principles, and the unorthodox for practicing the applications. The orthodox and unorthodox complement each other. When principles and applications are both perfected, you need never worry that your art is inferior to others.

Studying martial arts is not limited by age. Do not fear that your intelligence is not sufficient, but apply your mind diligently. Give it all your strength and do rest until you reach your goal. Confucius said: "If others can do one, I can do one hundred; if others can do ten, I can do a thousand." If you follow this path, even the ignorant will become enlightened, and the weak become strong. If you reflect on this calmly you will see its truth.

Among students of the martial arts, there are always boastful and vain types, who consider themselves to be very bright and claim to be able to master any art after seeing it just once. They do not realize it may seem that they can master it after seeing it once, but on closer observation they find they cannot. Thus martial arts principles are very profound and in no way comparable to a superficial understanding. Martial arts with unique postures are in no way comparable to the common. There are students who practice for many months without perfecting the postures and many years without understanding the principles. To say that one can master the martial arts in a single leap is simply impossible.

On the Twenty-Four Characters

Yin and yang are the ancestors of written characters and are prior to ch'i. "Yang" represents rising up, and in executing its postures, we must not pull ourselves up. "Yin" represents bending down, like clouds covering a mountain. It is not appropriate to discuss breathing techniques, but to speak in terms of rising and falling. "Supporting" represents holding up. "Halting" represents the balance of the ch'i. In "lifting" do not move. "Sinking" represents the ch'i gathering below. "Opening" represents being as joyful as a bobbing boat. "Entering" represents water rising to form clouds. In "exertion" the sinews rotate together. "Smashing" posture is like a smoking cannon. "Wounding" posture is exceedingly ferocious. "Splitting" sinews is like a knife chopping. "Pulling" posture is like pulling a rope. "Pushing" posture is like pushing a mountain. "Opposition" is straight and unbending. "Eating" posture is like wielding tongs. "Sticking" is not losing contact. "Following" is like a speeding star. "Evading" postures feature sinking to the side. "Startling" is like a crossbow bolt speeding from the string. "Hooking" postures are mostly bent. "Connecting" is like the fibers of the lotus root. "Advancing" is unstoppable. "Retreating" is like a coiling dragon. The sequence must not be confused, and the postures should be clearly distinguished. I entrust these words to posterity, but these secrets should not be recklessly transmitted.

Posture One: Presenting the Divine Peach of Immortality

A yin hand is extended out, and a yang hand drawn back
below the mouth.
The ch'i descends to the elbows.

The right foot is in front, and the left foot behind.

Two gentlemen enter the garden
And pluck the peach of immortality.
Both hands hold the peach palms up,
While the head is presented like a magnificent tower.

The "Yin" Posture

The peach of immortality from across the sea
appears only once in thousands of years. *Two yin hands
are extended out with light strength.*

Pluck the peach, glistening with fresh dew, at
dawn. *Withdraw the yang hands back below the mouth with
heavy strength.*

The air is balmy in the forest, as flowers brush the
face. *The left hand seizes, while the right hand, palm up, strikes
the face.*

The wind blows through the branches, and leaves cling to your body. *The left hand presses down, while the right chops, as you step into the opponent's crotch.*

Who can get the best of Tung-fang Shuo?[9] *Turn the elbow upside down, as the right hand strikes the opponent's privates.*

How could you be an idler, affecting the air of an imperial minister? *In seven stars posture, go down, turn up, and strike the opponent's mouth.*

Respectfully present with both hands as you stand by the precious Pool of the Immortals. *In turning stone stance, a yang fist is raised above the forehead.*

Joyfully wish the Queen Mother of the West a happy birthday. *After releasing, the fists are brought together and bound beneath the chest.*

In the forward facing "*Yin*" posture, the right foot is in front and the left in back. Both hands in yang position are extended bent in front of the chest. The ch'i of the elbows is drawn in and is jointly arrayed with the ch'i of the heart. The head drops downward with the ch'i sinking to the crown. Strike the Chest Center point (dan zhong, CV-17) at the lower end of the breastbone and the lower jaw.

Posture Two: Rhinoceros Gazing at the Moon

Turn the yin hand and push, as the head drops back and the ch'i sinks to the occiput.

The right foot is forward, and the left foot is back.

The rhinoceros can part the water,
Directly extending its two hooves.
Raising its head, it gazes
At the jade disc hanging in the west.

The "Yang" Posture

From birth, the rhinoceros communicates with heaven. *From birthday gift offering posture the two yang hands withdraw.*
Turning the head up to gaze at the bright moon, one ch'i connects the whole body. *As the two yin hands push outward, the head tilts back so that the face is looking up.*
Breathing hard but not tired, Ping Chi [10] inquires. *Withdraw the yang and release the yin, repeatedly breathing.*
Advance, straddling like you had slept with Lao tzu. *Eat the left hand, while the right leg rides on top of the upper arm.*

Hua Yüan[11] led his troops, wearing strong armor. *Stop the two hands and place them against the left flank, lifting the chest.*

Wen Ch'iao[12] burned the rhinoceros horn, illuminating the deep abyss. *Stand on the right foot, while the left foot is raised. The body bends forward. The forward hand is yang, and the rear hand is yin.*

A reflection is cast across the cold pool, while the frozen disc is still. *The reclining ox wags his head.*

Parting the water region has unsurpassed benefits. *The two hands grasp downward, and the two fists directly penetrate.*

The footwork faces forward as before. The two hands change to yin and extend directly forward. The head inclines forward, and the ch'i descends to the occiput, as you strike the navel.

Posture Three: Twin Rainbows Display Their Colors

The two hands form hooks with the backs facing up. Place them above the corners of the eyes. The ch'i rises to the backs of the hands.

The left foot is forward, and the right foot behind.

Auspicious rays suddenly arise,
And good fortune fills the long rainbows.
The five colors mount on high,
As twin bridges span empty space.

The "Supporting" Posture

Lao tzu, riding the ox, embraces the lord of the valley. *In moon gazing posture, the two hands push directly forward.*

Purple ch'i rises in brilliance, filling vast space. *This refers to one's own posture. Yin hands stick to the Greater Yang point in the temple.*

Immortal points the way, as clouds return to the mountain caves. *Assume cross hands posture.*

The crane soars up to heaven, and the bird escapes the cage. *Assume eagle posture.*

The Taoist priest observes the stars, examining the handle of the Big Dipper. *Raise the left hand high, while the right hand, back upward, is positioned under the arm.*

Su Ch'in[13] puts his sword on his back and divides male and female. *Turn around and bend forward, with the right hand in front and the left hand behind.*

A weak hand raises the cannon, while smoke and fire rises. *A hook hand, back up, strikes up at the bottom of the arm.*

The moon appears in the doorway, as the rainbows drop. *The two hands push forcefully. As the opponent is thrown, continue to pound his chest, hooking him fast.*

Facing forward, the two feet are side by side. The two elbows are bent, and the two hands stick to the area below the Greater Yang in the temple point. The ch'i rises, and the backs of the hands connect with the arms.

Posture Four: Immortal Carries Platter

A yin hand drops behind a yang elbow. Draw the ch'i back
and press down with the backs of the hands.

The left foot is in front, and the right foot behind.

The old one approaches the altar,
As light fills the jade platter.
The immortal's hand holds the platter firmly,
And the golden elixir rests within.

The "Halting" Posture

  The immortal on high approaches from afar,
sending down colorful clouds. *Assume cloud riding
posture. The yin hands bend into hooks and stick to the corner
of the eyes.*
  When this and that come together, is there no
reason? *Bow from the waist and bring the hands together.*
  The master salutes three times and welcomes his
honored guests. *In an attitude of yielding to the guest, the
two hands come forward in salute.*

Two dragons playing with their beads brush off the dust and dirt. *The two hands brush horizontally as if cleaning a surface.*

Singly straddle the basket like Master Han Hsiang.[14] *With your right hand grasp the opponent's right hand and lift his elbow, elevating his body.*

Carry the sword diagonally on your back like the immortal Lü Tung-pin.[15] *You can assume tiger straddling posture, but this is not as good putting the opponent's upper arm over your back.*

The medicine is complete on the golden platter, and the elixir is borne. *The hands, palm up, penetrate the chest.*

When one grain of elixir is swallowed, the ch'i enjoys eternal spring. *Bring the two hands together and lightly pat the area above the navel.*

The left foot is in front. The two hands turn yang and stiffly descend. The ch'i sinks to the backs of the ten fingers.

Posture Five: Monkey Offers Cup

The hands form as if holding a wine cup under the nose. The ch'i returns to the thumb and index finger.

The right foot is in front, and the left foot behind.

To drink this jade liquid
I offer you the golden cup.
I urge you to drink your fill
And become stinking drunk.

The "Startling" Posture

Holding the tray and bringing in the wine. *In tray holding posture, the two elbows are pulled back with the palms extended.*

Everything neat and orderly to the left and right, the banquet mat is spread. *As the two hands separate, the yin ch'i fully opens to the outside.*

I toast you, already holding two small cups. *Two hands thrust upward striking the opponent's nose.*

I urge you, sir, to drink a third cup. *Turn the body and strike him in the mouth.*

At the Pool of the Immortals you have imbibed the jade liquid. *Lift the face and swallow with the mouth.*

Climb that lofty mound and pour wine by the golden rampart. *Raise both hands above the head.*

Has the unstrained wine on top of the wall disappeared or not? *Bring the hands together and strike the head.*

Smell the fragrance, dismount your horse, and hurry up. *Roll up your sleeves, and in the attitude of tying up your horse, strike the opponent's face.*

From a forward posture, turn the body, so that the right foot is in front. The two hands scoop sideways as if holding a wine cup. The index finger springs up, while the ch'i of the little finger is stimulated and rises insistently, mounting to the arm.

Posture Six: Pair of Swallows in Flight

The body bends forward and the hands hang down. The hands scoop below the head. The ch'i travels in reverse to the toes.

The body turns, and the two feet are side by side.

The swallow spreads its wings,
With both wings hanging low.
Not like floating on water,
But like holding mud in its mouth.

The "Sinking" Posture

The sparrows return in pairs at springtime. *In cup offering posture, both hands penetrate upward, striking the face.*
Its feathers, in disarray, open one after another. *This refers to your own posture.*
With clouds high over the mountain, try your scissors for the first time. *Cross the hands and push the chest. The opponent will fall back face up.*
Purple clouds at the bottom of the sea, freely seize and eliminate. *Use lower penetration posture to strike the crotch.*

The king bids farewell before the hall and makes for his hideout. *In snake enters sparrow's nest posture, diagonally strike the opponent's throat.*

On the shore of rivers and lakes, they take mud in their mouths and return home. *In a posture suggestive of holding mud in the mouth, the left hand becomes yin and the right yang.*

Flower garlands fall to the water, fluttering and dancing. *In paired sparrow flying posture, the two hands stir evenly and descend all the way down.*

Flying on a clear autumn, jade is embraced. *In camel posture, strike the opponent's armpit with palm up.*

In forward posture, the two hands cast away. The toes of both feet are planted on the earth. Both hands droop sideways. Strike the Ghost Eye point (gui yan, SP-1) as the ch'i penetrates directly downward, entering the earth and locking down the big toe.

Posture Seven: White Goose Spreads Wings

The two hands separate, the two fists rise palms up, and the ch'i drops to the tips of the toes.

Stand on tiptoes.

A flock of geese on the sand
Are like so many white clouds.
Taking flight, they spread their wings
To escape the hunters.

The "Open" Posture

Cloud-white geese lie on the edge of the sand. *In swallow posture, bend forward and separate the two hands.*
Spreading their wings to take flight, they soar up to heaven. *From your own posture, strike at the opponent's nose.*
The shoulders separate horizontally as they spread their feather fans. *In camel posture, the hands separate.*
The two feet leap, and the fists descend. *Rise up as the two fists thrust downward.*

The scarlet phoenix preens its plumage. *In crossed hands raised at the gate posture, feint to the left and strike right.*

Purple swallow enters through the door, avoiding the curtains on either side. *In flying through the woods posture, the left hand blocks and the right hand strikes the flanks.*

The moment it becomes lax, the earth comes up fast. *In splitting Mount Hua posture, the right hand descends and pulls.*

When the goose leaves the cage, a whole flock returns. *Use both yin and yang hands in startled rabbit posture.*

Jump forward as the two hands separate, with the thumbs fanning out to the sides. If the opponent's elbows stick to his flanks, strike the flesh on the insides of the forearms.

Posture Eight: Fair Maiden Drills a Cave

Extend the arms, penetrating downward. Lower the head and
bend forward. The ch'i slides to the toes of the back foot.

The right foot is forward, and the left behind.

There is a rock at the mouth of the cave.
Drilling it, it becomes even stronger.
When the fair maiden arrives,
She advances with hands bound.

The "Entering" Posture

Turn the hands over and look up at the overhang-
ing stone cliff. *In wing spreading posture, the two fists
separately hump up.*

In the middle there is a small cave. *Clasp the two
hands, extending the index and middle fingers.*

The great general is brave, but conceals the back of
his neck. *As soon as the hands are released, both hands
penetrate the crotch and the head is lowered.*

The beautiful maiden, so quiet and modest, is

seemingly without shoulders. *Push forward with the face turned up.*

The hawk flies through the woods, seeking to move forward. *Step up and thrust with the hand, striking the throat.*

Six fabulous sea birds fly in retreat, regretting their inability to advance. *Reverse the diagonal foot and taking a step. Withdraw the hand.*

Raise the head, suddenly encountering a spacious area. *In stream jumping posture, turn the body and assume single whip.*

A beautiful girl wanders freely and sleeps peacefully. *This is your own posture.*

The body advances with the foot in front. The head is lowered. The two hands are extended straight out. The backs of the hands probing, strike the lower abdomen.

Posture Nine: Twin Dragons Dive into the Sea

The two hands are forcefully withdrawn and then pound down.
The ch'i rises to the tip of the middle finger.

The right foot is in front, and the left foot behind.

Seng Yao[16] drove the dragons
To break the walls and fly away.
When they dive into the sea in pairs,
Who can stop them?

The "Exertion" Posture

> The power of the dragon is yang and hard, but he
> conceals himself below. *In cave drilling posture, lower the*
> *head and step behind with the left foot.*
> The sea of suffering is boundless and its waters
> vast. *In sea probing posture, the left palm is yin and the right*
> *palm yang.*
> Touching the clear sky, it soars into the distance,
> and no one can stop it. *Exert yourself to the right and open*
> *the eyes wide.*

When the soaring claws come rushing, who would dare oppose it? *Exerting yourself to the left, shake the shoulder until the image spins before you, and then exert yourself forward. This is the secret.*

The flying claws rise up to the dark clouds. *Whip with the feet and pat with the hand.*

Wagging its tail, the green waves leap. *Curl the scorpion's tail and kick with the toes.*

Yeh Ch'a[17] sits upside down, as a thousand mountains shake. *Sitting cross-legged on the ground, the two hands press the earth.*

A hurricane kick reaches all the way to heaven. *Hurricane whip kick is followed by single whip.*

The left foot is in front. The two hands, in yin position, are extended straight out, as you take a step forward. The ch'i moves forward, as you strike below the opponent's breast.

Posture Ten: Powerful King Lifts Bronze Caldron

The two hands lift as you stand on your toes. The ch'i is drawn to the tip of the middle fingers.

The caldron stands for a thousand years,
Heavier than mountains and rivers.
The powerful king lifts it,
Pushing it up and away.

The "Smashing" Posture

> The King of Ch'u was a hero of his age. *Diving into the water posture.*
> With upturned face, an angry shout stirs up wind. *The two hands are placed below the underarms, as the head gazes up.*
> Palms down, the hands forcefully penetrate the earth. *Both hands press down.*
> The hands turn over, separate, and are held in space. *Both hands are raised over the head.*
> Twist three times, like harvesting mustard plants. *The left side is abruptly raised.*

Withdraw two steps to the right, like a flying wild
swan. *The right side is abruptly raised.*

Dark clouds cover the top and disperse from the
center. *Rotate horizontally.*

Eight thousand children pledge their full loyalty.
Lift up and look down.

Stand with the feet even. The fists are raised abruptly from
the crotch and are extended directly over the head. The ch'i
sinks to the point just above the first joint of the middle finger.
Strike troughs in the vessels.

Posture Eleven: Flying Goose Makes for Lake

Lower the head and place the hands behind the back. The ch'i shoots to the Vertex Gate (ding men, GV-22).

The right foot is in front, and the left foot behind.

The wild goose wings its way
Through the vastness of space.
Beating its wings up and down,
It makes for Lake Dongting.

The "Wounding" Posture

Deep in obscurity, they spread their wings and fly in a file. *From caldron lifting posture, shift to wild goose flying high.*

They leave their traces throughout the Five Lakes, whose waters are vast and boundless. *The hands separate, and the head is lowered, with the right foot in front.*

The hungry hawk dips its wings and chases the common birds. *The left hand is raised to strike the crotch. Use the back of the hand energetically.*

The scarlet phoenix preens its neck facing the sun. *The right hand chops down. From nest robbing posture thrust upward.*

The white egret extends its claws, eyeing the baby fish. *Dodge with the body in offering posture, with the palm up.*

The colorful ducks lower their heads and nibble rice and sorghum. *With a scissors movement, the right hand pressed down, and the head bends forward.*

Startled cold cries are choked over the shore of Hengyang. *Scissors back in reverse bridge mounting posture.*

They dive towards Lake Dongting, like libertines to a brothel. *Lower the head in cannon posture. The front hand is low, and the rear hand is high. Extend straight out in diagonal level body posture.*

Both hands brush, and then once again separate. The right foot steps into the opponent's crotch. The head butts forward. The ch'i descends to the Celestial Spirit point (tian ling, non channel), as you strike the Central Stomach Duct point (zhong wan, CV-12).

Posture Twelve: Precious Swords Both Split

The left knee is raised, and the two hands pat either side. The
ch'i reverts to one point.

The left foot is in front, and the right foot behind.

Sun Ch'üan[18] became enraged
And smashed the desk.
Lord Liu[19] drew his sword
And split the rock in two.

The "Splitting" Posture

      Su Ch'in rallied the six states and returned. *In lake
diving posture, the two hands are held behind the back, and the
head is lowered.*
      The precious swords are removed from their case
and brought down in a splitting motion. *This refers to
your own posture. The two hands strike down splitting.*
      When Hsiang Chuang[20] offers a drink, is this
without significance? *Clouds over crown posture.*
      Fan K'uai[21] began as a dog butcher, but was truly a
man of talent. *Mountain splitting posture.*

Chung Mou[22] split the dragon desk in anger. *Jump and whip with the feet, assuming flying horse mount posture.*

Madame loves to recline by her dressing table. *Tiger holds head in crossed hands posture.*

The rock fell into two halves under Liu Pang's sword. *Both hands pat, and the foot whips.*

Ch'ing Kung[23] comes along with Tzu Lung.[24] *Mountain shaking hidden sword posture.*

With both hands sideways, the knee is brought up, while the palms chop down. The ch'i of the thumb encourages the little finger, as you strike the opponent's wrist.

Posture Thirteen: Monkey Pulls Rope

Two hands tug at the head and then are lowered to the chest.
The ch'i penetrates the fingertips.

The left foot is in front, and the right foot in back.

There is a rope around the head,
Pulling this way and that.
The monkey tugs at it,
Falling and rolling over.

The "Pulling" Posture

> The precious swords split, using both hands. *In double splitting posture, the two little fingers use force to chop down.*
> The rope around the head is tightly tied. *This is your own posture. Grasp the two ears and pull down.*
> As straight as a red silk thread floating in the air. *Press down the wrist, moving forward and down.*
> As soft as red velvet hanging densely. *Lower again on the left, using sinking energy.*

Can the rope for drawing well water last forever?
Grab the face with the hand in body rising posture.

A single thread pulls for a thousand miles. *The two
hands dodge, then a plucking hand thrusts forward to press.*

The mythological monkey Sun Wu-k'ung pulls the
pig Chu Pa-chieh. *Two hands strike, landing a blow on the
head and retreating.*

One step, one fall, and behold the golden cicada.
*Pull down the head, lowering it past the crown. Fly across and
sit in the nest again.*

Both hands are held sideways, while the ch'i descends to
the ten fingertips, as they are folded in. The elbows are forcefully brought in to the chest. The body crouches down, and
the ch'i moves to the buttocks. Seize the opponent's arm.

Posture Fourteen: Two Hands Push Mountain

The hands are extended out from beneath the heart and press against the opponent's chest. The ch'i rushes to the center of the palm.

The right foot is in front, and the left foot behind.

Immovable your opponent,
And stable as Mount Tai.
Push him with two hands,
And he is violently lifted up.

The "Pushing" Posture

When the pulling posture is executed, the Pillar of Heaven is demolished. *In pulling rope posture, fiercely advance and go down.*

If the heel has no line, how can it be supported. *This is your own posture. Push with two hands.*

You are able to topple all the heroes of the age. *Catch the arm on the left side, sinking low.*

Eternal thoughts are stirred up. *Push the chest on the right side. Bring the palms together and separate them.*

Who says that Mount Tai is unshakable. *In tiger pouncing posture, the right thrusts and the left presses.*

When you lean like a rotten tree, how can you support yourself? *Turn the body and pull down. Execute flying immortal palm.*

Assassins burst through the curtains at the Yong-men banquet, while armed guards are sent sprawling.[25] *Push straight ahead with the left palm. The right palm opens to the rear.*

The orders of the invincible army of Yüeh Fei[26] may be taken as a model. *Turn your steps and push repeatedly with both hands.*

The backs of both hands stick to our chest and then rush forward. The ch'i emerges from the heart.

Posture Fifteen: Our Fate Arrives

The hands are crossed and the head lowered. Push forward forcefully.

The ch'i is exerted in the middle finger.

The left foot is forward, and the right behind.
Who can fathom Ch'i-men divination?
The Celestial Stem *chia* symbol may at any time
Arrive to deliver the fateful letters: Yin and yang.

The "Opposition" Posture

The messages of tun-chia divination are imponderable. *In pushing mountain posture, the body probes forward as if reading a book.*

Who knows the supreme joy of this process? *The two hands cross and push forward.*

Suddenly meeting an auspicious day, the Celestial Stem *jia* arrives. *Push on the left.*

Later this is followed by more good luck. *Push on the right.*

Yin and yang, for and against, observe the two extremes. *Step up and scissors. Assume twin dragons dive into the sea posture.*

The light of the sun, moon, and stars separates into the Celestial Stems *i, ping, ting. There are three "light" postures: left, right, and center.*

When you have free time, calm your mind and carefully play with it. *The right hand is sideways, the left hand extended, and the eyes examine closely.*

In predicting the spirits, they are very difficult to fool. *Cross your hands and butt forward, showing your face in space.*

Two yin hands connect and cross, and extended straight above, the head thrusts forward. The ch'i descends to the point just above the wrists, as you strike the chest and stomach.

Posture Sixteen: Fierce Tiger Bares Its Claws

Turn the body and make contact. The hands forcefully press down. The ch'i penetrates the center of the hand.

The two feet are placed together.

The fierce tiger rolls over
And uses all its power.
Penetrating into the very earth,
It immediately pounces.

The "Eating" Posture

Of all the animals, the tiger is most revered. *In delivering letter posture, cross the hands and penetrate forward.*
When the tiger is hungry, it prowls for food at Zhenshanmen. *This refers to your own posture. Both hands are extended straight and press down.*
It ferociously chases a deer, extending its jade-like claws. *The two fists, one yin and one yang, thrust diagonally.*
When thirsty, it drinks from the green stream, revealing the golden basin. *The yin and yang hands separate.*

Putting up stubborn resistance at a strategic point in the wilds, a man loses his nerve. *Turn the body and stab at the elbow, as the left hand bends down.*

Cut its tail, and it retreats to the cave, scarred out of it's wits. *Assume reverse nest sitting posture, as the right side stamps.*

The wandering herd of sheep all lower their heads. *Both hands pull the head down, while the left knee is raised.*

Again the traveler does not dare to speak. *The hand pulls in the attitude of beckoning someone and returns to claw bearing posture.*

Stand with the feet parallel. Both hands are yin. The thumbs support from below, and the four fingers curl under like an iron column. Seize the opponent's wrist.

Posture Seventeen: Chung K'ui Rubs His Forehead

The right fist is held palm up, and the left fist is placed just above the heart. The ch'i concentrates in the Vertex Gate.

The right foot is in front, and the left foot behind.

The deity Chung K'ui[27] brings peace to the home.
The two hands polish and rub.
By rubbing the forehead,
All evil demons are scarred away.

The "Sticking" Posture

Guarding the Central Palace in high spirits. *In claw barring posture, stare angrily with the eyes.*

Imposing in stature, he reveals a spiritual aura. *This refers to your own posture. One hand is above and the other below.*

Indirectly hastening to the golden steps and wiping out waste. *The left hand rises upright, while the right hand is positioned horizontally beside the flank.*

Withdraw the jade flute and sachet. *Assume canon at the head posture.*

He has risen up to the clouds and stood at the gates of the Emperor of Heaven. *In forehead rubbing posture, the body bends forward with the left hand above and the right below.*

As top successful candidate, he is appointed an official in Hades. *Assume God of Literature raises dipper posture.*

The green-robed officials, arrayed below, hold their swords. *The body moves back and forth, as the hands are raised above the head.*

Pacifying the evil demons, they hold their heads and hide. *Assume tiger holds head posture.*

Both hands are held sideways and close to the ears. Then they are carried behind the body as the head inclines backward. The right hand pushes up in ward-off and is positioned just above the head. The left hand sticks to the left flank. The head thrusts up while remaining enclosed by the arm.

Posture Eighteen: Concealed Crossbow Shoots Eagle

The right hand rolls down, while the left hand thrusts up. The ch'i is gathered in the channel troughs.

The right foot is in front, and the left foot in back.

Of all the birds flying in the air,
The eagle is most difficult to hit.
But when the concealed crossbow shoots,
The eagle has no defense.

The "Following" Posture

Throw up a blind and steal a peak. *In forehead rubbing posture, the eyes look up.*

Up in the sky, scraping heaven, a fabulous black bird. *This is your own posture. Use trough hand method to shoot upward.*

The right hand releases the arrow that strikes with destructive force. *Like a cannon pounding heaven, the left hand pulls the opponent down, while the right hand strikes the nose.*

The left hand holds the bow, that is already prepared. *In ax splits Lao tzu's hall posture, the right hand splits, and the left hand pushes the chest.*

The great bird spreads its wings, but finds no safe haven. *Bend the bow, and stepping up with the right foot, strike the face.*

Shoot the falcon from the high wall, as colored feathers rain down. *Step forward with the left foot and strike with concealed hand.*

The ten fingers join the bow, and all shoot up together. *Turn the head and assume fierce tiger turns body posture, using the* chih 知 *character hand technique.*

Even the flying tiger could not escape this attack. *Draw back to the chest and maintain revert to source posture. Then penetrate the opponent's heart with a flaming arrow.*

Both hands are held with the palms facing the body. The tip of the middle finger of one hand thrusts directly up, while the ch'i of the other elbow is drawn down and penetrates to the armpit.

Posture Nineteen: White Tiger Leans on Mountain

The two hands open out laterally, while the body leans backward. The ch'i flashes in the back.

The left foot is in front, and the right foot in back.

The white tiger washes its face,
Relaxes its body and rolls over.
As the two palms face up,
The weight of Mount Tai bears on a single egg.

The "Evasion" Posture

> Hide in ambush, bend the bow, and wait for the prey. *Assume eagle shooting posture.*
> With one jump, white tiger enters the deep mountains. *This refers to your own posture.*
> Turn the body and stand erect on the high mound. *Raise both hands and press with the back.*
> Lower the head, bend down, and gaze at the blue water straits. *The right foot is inserted backward, and the right hand strikes the belly.*

Spread your flying wings and expand your feathers. *The body assumes striding tiger climbs mountain posture.*

Close the mouth of the dipper and display its splendor. *When you clap the hands, the tiger's jaws are brought together.*

Barring its teeth and gesturing with its claws, it backs into its lair. *Turn the body and scissors, separating the hands to the left and right.*

Twisting the neck and holding the head is no casual thing. *Turn the body and move diagonally, executing withdraw cannon fist posture.*

One foot is in front and one foot behind. The head tilts backward and the hands dodge to the rear. The ch'i descends to the backs of the hands, and the head ch'i sinks to the occiput.

Posture Twenty: Twin Peaks Face Each Other

Both elbows rise together and are brought in to the chest, with the elbows facing out. The ch'i is concentrated in the points of the elbows.

The right foot is in front, and the left behind.

By the old ford at Jade Gate,
Twin peaks are in plain view.
The points of the elbows rise vertically,
As you strike the heart.

The "Startling" Posture

>   Turn your back to the Taihang Mountains and
> gaze at the Jade Gate. *Assume mountain leaning posture.*
>   Twin Peaks face each other in a posture of self-
> respect. *This refers to your own posture.*
>   Ch'en Hsiang[28] wields a splitting ax, and Mount Hua
> crumbles. *The right hand chops the elbow, and the left hand strikes.*
>   Pan Ch'ao[29] entered the pass and preserved the
> ferry crossing. *The left elbow turns, as you step up to the left.*
> *Use the technique of sticking to the opponent and leaning.*

Under the bright moon of autumn, pound with the frosted pestle. *Step up with the right foot, as the right elbow presses down.*

At midnight on the mountain top, the ape cries from the heart. *Scissors with the arms and raise the body. Pluck the opponent's ears and pull down.*

Heaven creates, earth establishes, and historical relics remain. *Tease with the elbow in white tiger washes face posture.*

Heaven and earth have existed from time immemorial. *Both elbows shake in spinning windlass posture.*

Both wrists bend and are hooked at the sides of the center of the chest. The points of the elbows are thrust forward. The ch'i descends just above the elbow joints as you strike the opponent's flank.

Posture Twenty-One: Crab Joins Its Claws

The two hands circle to the outside and come together to strike the Greater Yang point in the temples. The ch'i piles up in the middle finger.

The crab salutes with its pincers,
A pair of golden claws.
When they come together in the middle,
Your skull will be smashed.

The "Hooking" Posture

The crab spits saliva without exposing its head. *Assume facing posture.*

Act with reckless abandon and total freedom. *Wage warfare with both hands. Penetrate from the right.*

Carry a wolf's claw on the right, like an eagle feather arrow. *Chop with the right hand that cuts right through.*

The left hip bends like a crescent moon in autumn. *Step up to the left, bring the hands together, and draw the bow again.*

The cannon on the inside first strikes the ears. *The left hand strikes the left ear, and the right hand the right ear.*

Yin and yang grind against each other, turning forever and ever. *Expand the palms outward and strike the ears and cheeks. Withdraw and strike the nose and mouth.*

When the crab meets an opponent, it salutes with its two claws. *The two hands strike the opponent's head and ears.*

When the whole body is covered with armor and helmet, you will never have problems. *Draw the opponent's chest, remaining in joined claws posture.*

Both hands are yin. From the outside they close in. The ch'i descends to the joints of the ten fingers. Strike the Greater Yang point in the temple.

Posture Twenty-Two: Young Boy Worships the Buddha

Rolling hand penetrates the opponent's nose and mouth, with the backs pressed together. The ch'i rises to the ten fingertips.

The right foot is in front, and the left hand behind.

The virtuous youth
Pays his respects to Kuanyin.[30]
Devoted to Amitabha,[31]
Red fire emerges from the forest.

The "Connecting" Posture

The female demon is the red child. *Uniting nails posture.*

The Mahasattva[32] touches others with the teachings, perfecting their virtue. *The two palms are joined, and then you perform the kowtow.*

Kneel down, bow the head, and seal the anus. *The hands separate and descend, as two fists penetrate. Kneel down on the right knee, maintaining the left vertical. The right fist pounds the opponent's foot.*

Rising up, raise the pearl, as the gates of heaven swing open. *Turn the body, press the palms together, and strike the opponent's face.*

Gaze at Manjusri[33] on the left, and slip away on the right. *From the "following" posture, turn to the left and join the palms.*

Look at the bodhisattva Samantabhadra,[34©] who is coming on the right. *Turn the body to the right and join the palms.*

A cloud of fire dances in the sky. *The joined hands are raised and separated one at a time.*

Worship at the Lotus Tower with twenty-four obeisances. *Join the hands and repeatedly touch the head.*

Press the palms of the hands together like a Buddhist worshipping the Buddha. As you thrust them upward, the ch'i settles in the ten fingertips and rises to the tip of the nose.

Posture Twenty-Three: Butterflies Flying Side By Side

The backs of the hands are pressed together. Extend the fingers and pound the chest. The ch'i is urged to the fingertips.

The right foot is in front, and the left behind.

The butterflies sport among the flowers,
Flying slowly towards us.
In Chuang tzu's dream,[35]
They play together in the plum blossoms.

The "Advancing" Posture

Do not worry that the butterfly's strength is slight. *Bring the hands together and strike the chest.*
Feeding the whole morning, a pair of golden door leaves. *Cross the hands and penetrate.*
When spring comes to the region south of the Yellow River, the flowers bloom profusely. *The right hand is rigid, and the left teases. Then the right strikes the abdomen.*
Rain beats the Yangzi River in autumn, as the leaves become luxuriant. *Step up on the right and strike with a chop.*

All the children play joyfully and clap their hands together. *Step up on the left and protect the ears. The right palm slaps.*

Dancing wings, self-possessed and spontaneous. *Turn the body and slap with both hands.*

Only Chuang tzu's dream is most beautiful. *From the middle of the chest, the hands separate and move outward.*

At every moment the butterflies fly together. *The hands move down rigidly, the backs of the hands are brought together and penetrate.*

The backs of the hands are pressed together. They first descend, then ascend again to strike the opponent's throat.

Posture Twenty-Four: Golden Cat Catches Mouse

Use hurricane leg cross. Both hands hook to the outside. The ch'i is focused in the eyes.

Lower the body and cross the legs.

The real mouse
Always fears the cat.
With three wags of the cat's tail,
It will be difficult for the mouse to escape with its life.

The "Retreating" Posture

> Golden cat, golden tail, and golden yellow eyes.
> *Pair flying posture.*
> Golden eyes keep watch, while the mouse runs about busily. *Both hands are held vertically and then strike down at the left ear.*
> When a crossed hands chop arrives, the chest collapses. *Brush with both hands, and then strike the opponent's flank.*
> When you clutch the opponent, his shoulders and back will suffer. *Grab the right shoulder and sink down.*

Turn the body and jump directly into the garden on the west. *Turn the body and jump, assuming fruit gazing posture.*

Once again the claws sweep the neighbor's wall on the east. *Assume tiger riding posture, as the right foot sweeps.*

When you attack head on, the hordes of mice all perish. *Bend the body and pound the opponent's head.*

Casually withdraw from your meal and linger without purpose. *Execute three turning steps, and in "moving" character posture, close the form.*

The two hands fly together and turn to the back. Both legs twist. As the two hands become yin, they separate and move to the outside. Both wrists and elbows are bent. The ch'i lands in the Vertex Gate point, toes, hips, elbows, and fingertips, as we assume an attitude of surveying prospects.

The Twenty-Four Unorthodox Postures

1. "Yin": Liu Hai Plays with Moon Toad

The two fists are opposite each other, and with the arms bent, are held beneath the ears. The ch'i of the elbows sinks to the left and right sides of the abdomen. The head bends forward, or the arms block to the inside or outside.

2. "Yang": Push the Boat Forward

The two hands turn palms outward and forcefully thrust upward. The head inclines backward, and the ch'i sinks to the occiput. Strike the root of the opponent's thigh.

3. "Supporting": Soft Hand Raises Cannon

The hands form hooks and stick to the corners of the eyes. The ch'i is raised to the backs of the hands, as you strike the jaw.

4. "Halting": Old Peasant Turns Winnowing Basket

Both hands turn yang, one long and one short. Thumbs rotate to the outside, as you press the opponent's arms.

5. "Raising": Snake Enters Sparrow's Nest

Both hands turn yin and execute an upward ward-off. As the little finger turns up, the rear hand turns yang and thrusts upward. The ch'i sinks to the first joint of the middle finger, as you strike the opponent's chest.

6. "Sinking": Seeking a Pearl in Turbid Water

Both hands press down sideways, as the thumbs urge the little
fingers. The feet are raised one after the other, and the head
bends forward. The ch'i sinks to the corners of the forehead,
as you press the backs of the opponent's hands.

7. "Open": Two Maidens Hold Silkworms

You can use either both hands yang, or one yin and one yang.
The little finger urges the thumb, as the hands sweep to the
outside; or with hands in yin posture, the thumbs urge the
little fingers, as the hands sweep to the outside. Straighten the
wrists.

8. "Entering": Seeking a Cub in a Tiger's Lair

The hands become yin, as the ch'i sinks to the first joint of the
middle finger. The head bends forward, with the ch'i sinking
to the Vertex Gate. Strike the area beside the opponent's
breast.

9. "Exertion": Twin Dragons Herd Horses

Both hands are yin. As we inch forward, the ch'i emerges
three times and enters three times. Strike the opponent's lower
ribs.

10. "Collapse": Smashing Stone Startles Heaven

Stand with the feet together and one hand sideways. With the
ch'i of the thumb leading, the hand rises from the inner side
of the crotch. The rear hand goes to the front arm and slaps
with great force, collapsing the opponents channel trough.

11. "Wounding": Purple Swallow Flies Through Woods

The front arm sticks crosswise to the breasts, while the rear hand is hooked and placed reversed beside the rear hip. The index, thumb, and little fingers of the front hand are both bent. The three fingers swipe straight ahead, while the rear hand swings up and remains solidly in place. The front hand is aligned with the rear hand and slaps the opponent's channels. Like thunder shaking the earth, strike his abdomen.

12. "Splitting": Draw Sword and Sever Snake

In crossed legs stance, the front hand is yang and is raised up from below. The rear hand rises straight up and splits sideways in front. The thumb urges the little finger as you chop down. The ch'i of the front hand sinks to the first joint of the middle finger or the tip of the little finger. Strike a pressure point on the back of the upper arm.

13. "Pulling": Fierce Tiger Backs into Corner

Both hands attach to the opponent's wrists. The head bends forward, and the corners of the forehead sink down. The ch'i concentrates in the back of the buttocks, as you grasp the opponent's wrists.

14. "Pushing": Iron Fan Lingers in Doorway

Both hands are held sideways as they grasp the opponent's shoulders and push forward. The ch'i sinks to the ten fingertips.

15. "Opposing": Galloping on Horseback and Weilding a Sword

Both hands become yin as the "tiger's mouths" cover tightly and move horizontally to the inside. The power of the thumbs is activated as you seize the opponent's wrists.

16. "Eating": White Snake Coils Around Vine

One yin hand uses the "tiger's mouth" to seize the opponent's thumb. When you take his thumb, as the liver ch'i of your hand enters and the feet sink, your strength will be tenfold. Squeeze the opponent's wrists.

17. "Sticking": Indra Twists the Lock

The two palms are brought together, one above and one below. The little finger of the top hand moves toward the inside, sticking to the hollow of the opponent's shoulder. The thumb of the rear hand is drawn to the center of the chest. Exchanging left and right, you lean on the opponent's channel troughs.

18. "Following": Red Robed Emperor Nods His Head

The front hand grabs the opponent's hand. Rush forward scissoring up, as the rear hand pecks the Vertex Gate. The ch'i sinks to the five finger tips. Strike the forehead and skull.

19. "Evading": Kuanyin Presents Palms

The front hand is held sideways and erect in front of the hollows of the shoulders. The rear hand is extended straight out close to the rear hip. One foot is in front, as you assume cross posture. The ch'i of the little finger of the front hand travels to the breast, while the ch'i of the rear hand travels to the fingertips. Advance on the opponent's front hip, and with rapid steps strike his private parts.

20. "Startling": Golden Buckle and Jade Pendants

Both arms bend upward as the body turns. The rear leg sweeps, and the ch'i travels to the five fingertips. The kidney ch'i encourages the heart ch'i. Either take to your heels or stamp on the sternum.

21. "Hooking": Leading an Ox to Court

Both hands are yin, and the ten fingers dig down. The elbows are bent and immobilize the opponent's arms and toes. Your thumb blocks his feet, and your knees, facing his legs, bend.

22. "Connecting": Chang Fei Drives the Horses

Both hands are yang. Bend the elbows and press down on the opponent's arms. Your front foot is lifted and then placed down, blocking the opponent's heel. The hands change to yin and push the opponent's face. Your rear hand may hold either the back of his head or his hair.

23. "Advancing": Secretly Crossing the Ford at Chencang

The front hand is held sideways, as you kick the opponent's crotch. The rear hand drills straight ahead for the abdomen. You need to charge with fast feet.

24. "Retreating": Gazing at Fruit on Mount Hua

The two hands turn and the body sweeps. Turn again and sweep again. One shoulder is elevated and the other lowered; one hip is raised and the other sinks. Turn the body and look up, as both arms bend, with one held close to the area below the ear.

Although these are unorthodox postures, they cannot be ignored. We first cultivate the orthodox, but in practice we most often use the unorthodox. The orthodox are for the most part stiff, but the unorthodox are more lively. The orthodox are expansive, whereas the unorthodox are contracted and well adapted to advancing, retreating, and transforming. For this reason I have included them at the end for reader's edification.

5

Conclusion

China's humiliating defeat by Japan in the Sino-Japanese War of 1894 exposed the superficiality of court sponsored experiments in modernizing industry, education, and the military. Radical reformers argued for a more sweeping cultural shift. In his 1896 *Jen hsüeh* (Study of benevolence), T'an Ssu-t'ung highlighted the need for reviving the spirit of knight-errantry. K'ang Yu-wei in his 1884 *Ta-t'ung shu* (Book of the Great Unity) and memorials to the throne called for a nation of "citizen soldiers." K'ang's vision for a new China emphasized three areas of education: moral, intellectual, and physical, and of these, physical education was the most appropriate for children: "Their academic burden should be somewhat decreased, and their play increased, in order to stimulate their ch'i and blood and develop their bodies."[1] There is a tone of extreme urgency in all of these late nineteenth century reformers and a belief that the health of the body politic begins with the health of the body.

In its early phase, late nineteenth century reform ideology forefronted progressive tendencies in traditional Chinese thought as a rationale for change, but increasingly, with the founding of the Republic in 1911, there were voices calling for total Westernization. When Liang Ch'i-ch'ao says in his 1916 *Chung-kuo chih wu-shih-tao* (Chinese bushido): "The martial spirit ends where autocratic rule begins,"[2] he speculates that the martial spirit, mobilized to expand and defend the empire, was deliberately stifled by elites to lessen the threat to their domestic autocratic rule. K'ang and Liang were extremely impressed with physical education in Germany and Japan and advocated Western calisthenics and military style exercises in the schools. In a 30,00 character long chapter entitled "Lun shang-wu" (On promoting the martial spirit) in his *Hsin-min shuo* (The new citizen), Liang expounds on the Spartan ideal of citizen soldiers and calls for its adoption as a model for China. This theme was taken up and implemented in the teens of the twentieth century by China's foremost educators Ts'ai Yüan-p'ei and his successor Fan Yüan-lien, who saw China squeezed between the competing designs of Western and Japanese imperialists. It was in this life-and-death atmosphere that t'ai-chi ch'üan emerged from the shadows in the first decades of the twentieth century, and through mass publications and state and privately sponsored martial arts institutes, began to reach a national audience.

It may well be that the movement to promote Chinese martial arts as a national treasure during this period was in part a reaction against Western calisthenics. The assertion of the superiority of Chinese physical culture and martial arts is a persistent undercurrent in the prefaces to innumerable books on t'ai-chi ch'üan from the turn of the century on. Chou Lin-I puts it this way: "Although Western physical culture understands the significance of developing our physical natures for fulfilling life, it is still at a very superficial stage when it comes to the essence and function of natural movement."[3] Answering the common criticism that physical education had become irrelevant in the era of modern weaponry, Chiang Ying-hua stated in the *Kuo-shu chou-k'an* (Martial arts weekly), founded in 1928 as the organ of the Central Martial Arts Institute:

> Although modern weapons have replaced martial arts, Euro-peans and Americans still practice, study, and promote them for body and mind. Even their games embody the martial spirit, while we Chinese look down on the martial arts. . . . and therefore abandon our tradition in hopes of imitating others. Before we have mastered Western ways, we have already earned the title of "the sick man of Asia." We fail to understand that a healthy spirit is a function of a healthy body, and only with a healthy citizenry can we have a healthy nation. Although

martial arts are not relevant to every aspect of modern warfare, they are useful in strengthening the individual, training groups, creating courageous soldiers, and developing responsibility and stamina. Is this less important than studying bombers, warships, artillery, and poison gas?[4]

This echoes four centuries later the same sentiments we found in Ch'i Chi-kuang and his fellow military strategiests as they attempted to rally patriotic resistance in the sixteenth century.

The martial arts movement was forced to defend itself both against the notion that any physical education was irrelevant for modern warfare on the one hand and that Western physical education was superior on the other. National identity is an important ingredient in the will to resist, and national identity was threatened by Westernization. The transition from peasant in the Chinese empire to citizen of the Chinese nation was not smooth or simple, and the possibility that the "Mandate of Heaven" could fall into foreign hands was not unthinkable. Why bother to resist Western imperialism if you yourself are becoming Westernized? China could not win by losing her soul. The century from the Opium Wars (1839–42, 1856–60), through the Sino-Japanese war of 1894, to the War of Resistance (1937–45) was one when national defense was paramount in the minds of statesmen and ideologues. During this prolonged crisis, poetry, calligraphy, and painting could not carry the banner of Chinese culture and national identity. What could China construct to stand up to the Japanese national mythos of a divine emperor and the samurai *bushido*? After all, Japan was able to combine thoroughly Western militarization with the ancient code of the warrior. T'ai-chi was the most distinctively Chinese of all the martial arts, and with the creation of a patriotic lineage, it was well positioned to play the role of vehicle for reviving the Chinese martial spirit. No less a figure than Chiang Kai-shek says in the pages of the *Kuo-shu chou-k'an*:

Our 5000 year old nation, once the mightiest in the world, has now fallen to the status of semi-colonialism. Although we are in cultural decline, economic stagnation, and are politically, socially, and commercially backward, our citizen's neglect of physical education, lack of training, and loss of competitiveness are really the most important causes. . . . Chinese martial arts are the most effective method for strengthening the body and were the creation of our ancient sages. Its methods are extraordinary; the agility and quickness of its postures, and the subtlety of its escapes and strikes cannot be equaled by any other nation.[5]

Cheng Man-ch'ing unites the themes of self-strengthening and the superiority of Chinese physical culture, and adds a new one—China's contribution to world culture:

Modern medicine knows only about breathing, but nothing about ch'i; knows only about the diaphragm, but nothing about the tan-t'ien; knows only about the contraction and relaxation of the muscles, but nothing about the function of the ch'i dynamic potential; knows only about strengthening the sinews and joints to make them strong and flexible, but nothing about strengthening the seminal essence and supplementing the marrow; knows only about nervous sensation and perception, but nothing about the subtleties of spiritual reactions; knows only about the circulation of blood and cell metabolism, but nothing about the engendering and restraining principle of the five phases, or the differences between yin and yang, waxing and waning. . . . In 1937 during the War of Resistance, I was in charge of the Hunan Provincial Martial Arts Institute, and t'ai-chi ch'üan played an important role in the curriculum for teaching soldiers, police, and ordinary citizens . . . . Not only do I hope to use t'ai-chi to strengthen the Chinese race and nation, but spread its benefits to the whole world.[6]

As anti-feudal skepticism peaked during the May Fourth Movement of 1919, and calls for total Westernization increased in some quarters, traditional Chinese martial arts fell under the stigma of "noxious residues of feudalism." With Western physical culture infiltrating the progressive school curricula, thinking on the role of the martial arts in the emerging society split into three approaches: abolition, reformation, and tradition. Reflecting on the vicissitudes of his personal journey towards a "correct" interpretation of t'ai-chi's origins and development, Huang Wen-shan in the Chinese language addenda to his 1973 *Fundamentals of Tai Chi Ch'uan* says:

> During the 1920s, T'ang Hao and Hsü Chen, under the influence of May Fourth Movement skepticism, advocated using scientific methods to rid t'ai-chi history of mythological and superstitious elements. . . . In 1932, when T'ang personally went to Ch'en village, he discovered that the Ch'en family manuals said nothing about t'ai-chi's origins, much less Chang San-feng, and thus concluded that traditional views were all bogus. . . . As a result, he concluded that t'ai-chi ch'üan was a product of folk culture and of a long period of development. We can happily accept the latter conclusion, but he denies the role of Chang San-feng and believes that Wang Tsung-yüeh belonged to the Ch'ien-lung period (1736-95). . . . Ten years ago when I was drafting the manuscript for this book, I too was under the influence of his theory.[7]

Huang goes on to criticize a number of T'ang's points and to seek to rehabilitate Chang San-feng. Although in past studies I have critically examined many of T'ang's assumptions, they are not nearly so naive as Huang's criticisms. What underlies both Huang and Cheng's discomfiture is the notion that an undistinguished family in a backwater village could have produced a sophisticated art, and that this interpretation came to be officially embraced by a government from which they had fled into exile. A return to traditionalism can only be understood in the context of anti-communism and the Cold War, as their arguments make no pretense to observing scholarly norms. Cheng expressed the traditionalists' view:

> Some people spare no effort in making slanderous claims that
> the immortal Chang San-feng was not the creator of t'ai-chi
> ch'üan. I have no idea what their motivation is. In former
> times, t'ai-chi ch'üan was supreme among the martial arts. At
> that time, warfare still relied heavily on the martial arts. . . .
> When I carefully examine the "Treatise on T'ai-chi ch'üan," I
> find it to be beautifully written and perfectly natural. Who
> could have attained this level? . . . . If not the likes of Chang
> San-feng and Lü Tung-pin, who could have accomplished this?[8]

What impressed Cheng so much that he felt he had no choice but to
attribute t'ai-chi ch'uan to a figure whom respected scholars like
Anna Seidel and Huang Chao-han barely believe existed, let alone
created t'ai-chi ch'üan? Surely it was the marvelous marriage of a
practical art with the highest principles of Taoist philosophy, military
strategy, meditation, and medicine. Ch'ang Nai-chou's writings demonstrate that this chemistry could be achieved in the eighteenth century
with no reference to Chang San-feng, Wu-tang, the Internal School,
Wang Tsung-yüeh, or t'ai-chi ch'üan. Whether this means that the
Ch'en family art shared these characteristics in the eighteenth century, or whether t'ai-chi acquired them in the late nineteenth and
early twentieth centuries cannot be proven with available documents.
We do, however, know for certain that martial arts history has been
an intense battleground for sectarian and political partisans, and that
forgery of documents and fabrication of history are accepted laws of
engagement. Myth is a powerful tool in mobilizing a people, and we
must never forget that propoganda was the overriding concern of all
those who have written her history—the rationalists no less than the
traditionalists. From the 1930s on, the left-right struggle—Communist
vs. Nationalist—was layered over the China vs. imperialist struggle
and colored everything in the intellectual as well as political arenas.
Both parties sought to appropriate the martial arts to stand up to
outside aggression, but each sought to cast it in accord with their
own ideology. Hence, KMT supporters like Cheng and Huang insisted

that it be projected as a divine gift of the sages and immortals, whereas those on the left, like T'ang Hao and Hsü Chen, sought to cast it as a product of the people and purge it of supernatural claims and secrecy.

Looking at t'ai-chi's ch'üan's construction and promotion in the early twentieth century in the context of the culture wars of the time compels us to also examine the debates among advocates of martial arts, physical education, and military training. In the early 1930s many Chinese intellectuals already wrote as if World War II and a life-and-death struggle with Japan were inevitable. Life expectancy in China was only thirty years, compared with fifty-nine for Japan, and politicians routinely lectured the nation on its lack of fitness and fighting spirit. Ch'en Tun-cheng advocated an inclusive approach to martial arts, physical education, and military training that would use the strengths of each to correct imbalances in the others. He believed that physical education could correct deficiencies in martial arts, military training could correct deficiencies in physical education, and martial arts could correct deficiencies in military training. Saving his most rhapsodic prose for the contributions of martial arts, he writes:

> Because of martial arts' infinite complexity, offensive and defensive capabilities, exteme agility, and near supernatural powers, it is virtually unfathomable. Moreover, martial artists are able not only to brave ice and snow and cross rivers and mountains, but are adept at carrying out all manner of tasks. Cold and hunger do not affect them, and they are quick to respond to injustice with a spirit of knight-errantry. This is especially necessary for our armed forces, and that is why we say that only martial arts training will produce a strong and courageous army.[9]

Ch'en's vision of the special role of traditional martial arts and a balanced approach to the three forms of physical culture proved to be prophetic and was adopted as policy by both Nationalist and Communist governments.

We have hints of the existence of soft-style techniques
and ch'i development in Ch'i Chi-kuang and the Internal School,
but with Ch'ang Nai-chou we have a fully mature synthesis of
martial arts with military strategy, medicine, and meditation.
All of the ingredients in this synthesis were themselves highly
developed long before Ch'i Chi-kuang's *Classic of Pugilism*, but
Ch'ang is our first complete record of the synthesis. In understanding the origins and nature of t'ai-chi ch'üan we can profit
more from authentic and relavant non-t'ai-chi works than from
spurious or highly suspicious works posing as authentic t'ai-
chi documents. In this latter category we must include the Ma
T'ung-wen edition of the classics, works attributed to Ch'en
Wang t'ing and Ch'en Ch'ang- hsing, Ch'en Hsin's *T'u-shuo*,
and the "Bookstall Classics." We do not even know for sure
who wrote the extant manuscripts of the classics and do not
have a scrap of paper in Wu Yü-hsiang's own hand. Yang
Ch'eng-fu's two books were ghost written, and it is clear that
words have been put into his mouth. It is hoped that the three
works brought together here will join the repository of primay
research materials on t'ai-chi ch'üan, and that a clearer picture
of the development of t'ai-chi in China will stimulate a deeper
examination of its meaning in Western culture today. Every
human activity is embedded in a narrative that gives it meaning
in our lives. T'ai-chi today in the West is an imported cultural
artifact in search of a narrative: sword or ploughshares; arche-
type of warrior or sage; ritual or psychodrama; therapy or
orientalist fantasy of mastership; a ch'i-kung in the body of a
martial art or a martial art in the body of a ch'i-kung. Understanding the constrcted nature of the t'ai-chi narrative in Chinese
culture may help us better polish the dust from our own mirror.

Abbreviations

CC	*Chen chi*	陣紀
CKWSS	*Chung-kuo wu-shu shih*	中國武術史
CKWSSL	*Chung-kuo wu-shu shih-lüeh*	中國武術史略
HTHCC	*Huang Tsung-hsi ch'üan-chi*	黃宗羲全集
KSCK	*Kuo-shu chou-k'an*	國術週刊
TCCK	*T'ai-chi ch'üan k'ao*	太極拳考
TCCS	*T'ai-chi ch'üan shu*	太極拳術

Notes

1. General Introduction

1. Yung, "Lun Chung-kuo wu-shu te meng-ya ho hsing-ch'eng, p. 57.
2. Chuang Chou, *Chuang tzu*, Tza-p'ien, "Shuo chien."
3. CKWSS, pp.140–41.
4. T'ang, "Ch'ing-tai ya-p'o hsia te wu-shih chi ch'i chu-tso," p. 2.

2. Ch'i Chi-kuang's Essentials of the Classic of Pugilism

Introduction

1. TCCK, p. 7.
2. Ibid., p. 8.
3. TCCS, p. 432.
4. TCCK, p. 21–22.
5. TCCS, p. 432–35.
6. TCCK, p. 24.
7. Yang, "Hsü yü shih," p. 46.
8. Ko, *Pao P'u tzu*, "Hsing p'in."
9. CKWSS, p.146.
10. Lo, "Tui Yü Ta-yu te *Chien ching* tsai t'an," pp. 6–8.
11. *Sun tzu ping-fa*, "Chün cheng."
12. Ibid., "Hsü shih."
13. Ibid., "Chün cheng."
14. Ho, *Chen chi*, p. 57.
15. *Sun tzu ping-fa*, "Ping shih."
16. Ho, *Chen chi*, p. 23.
17. Wei Liao, *Wei Liao tzu* in *Wu ching ch'i shu*, p. 197.

18. Ibid., p. 182.

19. *San lüeh* in *Wu ching ch'i shu,* p. 215.

20. Ho, *Chen chi,* pp. 82–84.

21. Ibid., p. 93.

22. T'ang, *Wu pien* in *Ssu-ku ch'üan-shu chen-pen,* 4, Vols. 133–35, pp. 91–93.

23. Hsün Ch'ing, *Hsü tzu,* "I ping."

24. CKWSSL, p. 16.

25. Cheng, *Chiang-nan ching-lüeh* in *Ssu-k'u ping-chia lei ts'ung-shu,* p. 10.

26. Ho, *Chen chi,* p. 23.

Translation

1. I agree with Ma Ming-ta ("Ch'i Chi-kuang *Ch'üan ching* tuan lun," *Chung-hua wu-shu*, 1985, 4 :32–35; 5: 25–26) that the *Chi-hsiao hsin-shu* chapter title, "Ch'üan ching chieh-yao p'ien," is integral and should not, as some contemporary commentators such as Shen Shou have argued, be divided into "Chüan ching" and "Chieh-yao p'ien."

2. Ma Ming-ta suggests punctuating this passage so as to yield two distinct arts: "Twenty-four Throws" and "Pat on Horse." Although his position is well argued, in the present context, "Pat on Horse" standing alone without a number is too stylistically jarring.

2. Documents on the Internal School

Introduction

1. HTHCC, "Chu Ching-huai hsien-sheng pa-shih shou hsü," Vol. 11, p. 68.

2. Ibid., "Meng tzu shih-shuo," Vol. 1, p. 52.

3. Ibid., "Chen-huan Chang fu-chün mu-chih ming," Vol. 11, p. 40.

4. Ibid., "Jui-yan kung shen-tao pei," Vol. 10, p. 225.

5. Ibid., "Lu Chou-ming mu-chih ming," Vol. 10, p. 295.

6. Ibid., "Jui-yan kung shen-tao pei," Vol. 10, p. 225.

7. Ibid., "Meng tzu shih-shuo," Vol. 1, p. 60.

8. Ibid., "Wan Tsu-sheng mu-chih ming," Vol. 10, pp. 473–74.

9. Huang Pai-chia, "Cheng-nan she-fa," in T'ang Hao, Nei-chia ch'üan-fa te yen-chiu, n.p.

10. HTHCC, "Lin San-chia chuan," Vol. 10, p. 545.

11. *Meng tzu,* "T'eng Wen kung," 2.

12. *Chuang tzu*, "T'ien tao."

13. HTHCC, "Meng tzu shih-shuo," Vol. 1, p. 59.

14. CKWSSL, p. 21.

15. Chao Erh-hsün, et al, ed., *Ch'ing-shih kao*, 512, pp. 2567–68.

16. Wu Wen-chung, *T'i-yü shih*, p. 302.

17. Sun Wen, "Min-tsu chu-i san chiang," in Wu Chih-ch'ing, *Kuo-shu li-lun kai-yao*, p. 34.

18. Sun Wen, "Ch'ing-wu pen-chi hsü," reproduced in *T'i-yü wen-shih* 1, 1988, p. 35.

Translations

1. Tang Hao in his *Nei-chia ch'üan-fa te yen-chiu* carefully analyzes the "points" mentioned in the three Internal School documents. Based on T'ang's analysis and my own research, and using Nigel Wiseman translations and WHO alpha-numeric notation, the following are identical with common acupuncture points: Jumping Round (GB-30), Pool at the Bend (LI-11), Union Valley (LI-4), Inner Pass (PC-6), and Three Li (arm, LI-10). T'ang points out that GB-30, located on the lateral aspect of the buttuck, is buffered by ample muscle and difficult to access, while LI-11, LI-4, PC-6, and LI-10 would require capturing and immo-bilizing the opponent's arm and applying considerable force. He finds little correspondence between medical indications and purported martial art's appli-cations. Finding a *p'ang-kuang* 膀胱, but no *p'ang-kuang hsüeh* 膀胱穴 in the medical literature, T'ang speculates that if this refers to the bladder itself, then a blow might well prove fatal and thus qualify it as a "death point." T'ang indicates that the "jaw dislocate" and "throat lock" are grappling techniques, and not points at all, and that the "toad" is unattested either as a point or martial arts technique. Of the five acupoints mentioned in the *Art of the Internal School*, four are located in the lower arm, whereas the great majority of pressure points in other martial arts sources are located on the head and torso. Perhaps these are subsumed under "death, mute, veritgo, and couphing points," but altogether the passage looks like a vague recollection on Huang Pai-chia's part.

2. The character *k'o* 科 that appears in all editions of Pai-chia's *Art of the Internal School* is incomprehensible, and there is no definition of the word that can be stretched to fit this context. For the sake of translation, I have no choice but to hazard an emendation and suggest that *k'o* 科 may well be a scribal or typesetting error for *tou* 抖.

3. Sang I was a courageous military man during the Sung who won honors for action against bandits and northern invaders.

4. Ch'ang Nai-chou's Writings on Martial Arts

Introduction

1. Li Ch'eng gives "1724–1783" for Ch'ang's dates, and one can only wonder what sources were available to him in 1986 that were not available to the editors of the *Sishui Gazeteer* in the 1800s.

2. Ch'en, "Ch'ang-chia ch'üan chih yüan-liu k'ao," pp. 33–35.

3. Li, "Ch'ang Nai-chou Ch'en-kou chih-yu," pp. 26–27.

4. Ch'en Hsin, *Ch'en-shih t'ai-chi ch'üan t'u-shuo*, p. 478.

5. T'ang, TCCK, p. 116.

6. Hsü, *Ch'ang-shih wu-chi shu*, p. 2.

7. Ch'en Hsin, *Ch'en-shih t'ai-chi ch'üan t'u-shuo*, pp. 408, 413.

Translation

1. The original, here, is so corrupt that I have taken the liberty of emending the three yang channels of the foot to conform with standard medical models. Hsü Chen provides some notes on textual problems, but they are spotty and do not address all of the errors in this passage.

2. The original says "bottom."

3. The original says "inside."

4. The original says "outside."

5. *Sun tzu ping-fa*, Chap. 1.

6. Ibid., Chap. 5.

7. Ibid., Chap. 7.

8. In the Chinese inner alchemy tradition, the "baby boy" (*ying-erh* 嬰兒) represents the seminal essence; the "beautiful maiden" (*ch'a-nü* 妊女) represents the heart's fire; and the "yellow match-maker" (*huang-p'o* 黃婆) represents the mind in its role of bringing the above together.

9. A wise minister who used humor to advise Emperor Wu of the Han.

10. Prime Minister under Emperor Hsüan of the Han who had protected the infant prince before he assumed the throne.

11. Hua Yüan was an actor in the violent struggles of the Spring and Autumn period during the Chou dynasty.

12. Wen Ch'iao was a military officer during the Chin (265–316) who was active in pacifying rebellions but declined posts at court. On his way home, he lit a rhinoceros horn torch to search for strange creatures in a deep crevace, an event celebrated in a poem by Li Po.

13. Su Ch'in offered his diplomatic services to the state of Ch'in during the Warring States period, but when rejected, he unified the remaining six states in an alliance against Ch'in that held for fifteen years. He was finally assasinated in the state of Ch'i.

14. Han Hsiang was one of the Eight Immortals of the T'ang.

15. Lü Tung-pin was another of the Eight Immortals of the T'ang.

16. I cannot identify this figure.

17. A monster in Chinese mythology.

18. Sun Ch'üan was the ruler of the state of Wu during the Three Kingdoms period who joined together with Liu Pei to defeat Ts'ao Ts'ao at Red Cliff.

19. Liu Pei was ruler of the state of Shu during the Three Kingdoms period.

20. Hsiang Chuang was the younger brother of Hsiang Yü who revolted against the Ch'in and was ultimately defeated by Liu Pang, the first emperor of the Han. When Pei Kung was bidding farewell to Hsiang Yü at Hangmen, Pei invited Yü to stay for a drink, whereupon Hsiang Chuang drew his sword and attacked Pei Kung.

21. Fan K'uai was a former dog butcher who became a military officer and aided Liu Pang in winning victories that led to the founding of the Han.

22. Chung Mou is the style of Sun Ch'üan.

23. I cannot identify this figure.

24. Tzu Lung was the style of Chao Yün, a Three Kingdoms period general from the state of Shu who prevailed against Ts'ao Ts'ao.

25. Liu Pang was the object of an assasination attempt at a banquet hosted by his rival Hsiang Yü. Liu emerged unscathed and went on to found the Han dynasty.

26. Yüeh Fei was a hero of the Sung dynasty who won many victories against the Tunguistic dynasty of the Chin during the twelfth and early thirteenth centuries. He was slandered and died in prision at the age of thirty-nine.

27. Chung K'ui is a diety who protects human beings from evil.

28. I cannot identify this figure.

29. Pan Ch'ao was the younger brother of Pan Ku, known for his exploits in the Western Region.

30. Kuan-yin is the Godess of Mercy, or the feminine form of Avalokitesvara Bodhisattva.

31. Amitabha is the Buddha of infinite qualities, revered in Mahayana Buddhism as Lord of the Pure Land of the West. He is also associated with light and eternal life.

32. A mahasattva is a great being, noble, or bodhisattva.

33. Manjusri is the Buddha of Wisdom and the left hand assistant of the Buddha.

34. Samantabhadra is the Buddha of Sagacity and the right hand assistant of the Buddha.

35. Chuang tzu dreamt that he was a butterfly. When he awoke, he did not know whether he was Chuang tzu dreaming that he was a butterfly or a butterfly dreaming that he was Chuang tzu.

5. Conclusion

1. Su, "Kang Yu-wei te t'i-yü ssu-hsiang chi ch'i ch'eng-yin," p. 50.
2. Liang, *Chung-kuo chih wu-shih-tao*, p. 9.
3. Chou, "Lao tzu ssu-hsiang yü t'i-yü pen-chih," p. 49.
4. Chiang Ying-hua, *Kuo-shu chou-k'an*, 12–23, , 1934, no. 135, p.3.
5. Chiang Kai-shek, *Kuo-shu chou-k'an*, 3, 18, 1934, no. 113, p. 3.
6. Cheng, *T'ai-chi ch'üan tzu-hsiu hsin-fa*, pp. 22–23, 61.
7. Huang, *Fundamentals of T'ai Chi Chuan*, pp. 514–15.
8. Cheng, *T'ai-chi ch'üan tzu-hsiu hsin-fa*, p. 20.
9. Ch'en, *Kuo-shu chou-k'an*, 6,12, 1945, no. 168, p. 3.

Bibliography

Anon. *Ch'üan ching* 拳經 (Martial arts classics). Shanghai: Ta-sheng shu-chü, 1918; reprint, T'ien-chin shih ku-chi shu-tien, 1987.

Ch'ai Ju-chu 柴如柱. "Ju ch'üan-shih Ch'ang Nai-chou" 儒拳師萇乃周 (Ch'ang Nai-chou: scholar and martial arts master). *T'i-yü chi-k'an*, 1, (1921).

Chang Hsi-ching 張西京. "*Chien-ching* kuan-k'ui i-te" 劍經管窺一得 (A glimpse of the *Classic of Swordsmanship*). *Chung-hua wu-shu*, 3 (1985): 36.

Chang Hsüan-hui 張選惠. "Chen-kui te shih-liao: hsin-chin fa-hsien Ming k'o-pen *Wu-pei yao-lüeh*" 珍貴的史料新近發現明刻本武備要略 (Precious research materials: Ming edition of the *Wu-pei yao-lüeh* recently discovered). *Chung-hua wu-shu*, 6 (1988): 34–35.

Chang I 張誼 and Ch'e Ming-kui 車明貴. "Wu-ou yu-tu chüeh i-ch'an nei-chia ch'üeh yu liu lu ch'üan" 無偶有獨掘遺產內家確有六路拳 (A unique legacy: the Internal School's Six Paths still exists). *Wu-lin*, 5 (1984): 32.

Chang I-ching 張義敬. "T'ai-chi ching-chieh tsa-t'an" 太極境界雜談 (Random notes on the world of t'ai-chi ch'üan). *Wu-shu chien-shen*, 6 (1991): 14–15.

———. "Tsai-t'an nei-wai yu pieh" 再談內外有別 (A further discussion of the difference between the internal and external in the martial arts). *Wu-shu chien-shen*, 6 (1988): 10.

Chang Ju-an 張如安. "Nei-chia ch'üan ta-shih Chang Sung-hsi sheng-p'ing pien-wu" 內家拳大師張松溪生平辨誤 (Correcting errors in the biography of Internal School master, Chang Sung-hsi). *T'i-yü wen-shih*, 4 (1988): 28–30.

Chang Shu-hsien 張淑賢. "T'i-ch'ang wu-shu chuang wo Chung-hua: Chang Chih-chiang te wu-shu ssu-hsiang ch'u-t'an" 提倡武術壯我中華張之江的武術思想初探 (Promote martial arts and strengthen China: a preliminary examination of the martial arts thought of Chang Chih-chiang). *T'i-yü wen-shih*, 6 (1988): 32–34.

Chang Ssu-chung 張斯忠. "Ch'ing-jen Shen Fu p'ing-lun t'ai-chi ch'üan" 清
人沈復評論太極拳 (Ch'ing period literary figure Shen Fu's evaluation
of t'ai-chi ch'üan). *Wu-tang*, 1 (1990): 31.

Chang Tun-hsi 張敦熙. "T'ai-chi ch'üan fa-chan yü chu-shu" 太極拳發展
與著述 (T'ai-chi ch'üan's development and writings). In *Chung-kuo wu-shu
shih-liao chi-k'an*, Vol. 2 (1975): 46–52.

———. T'ai-chi ch'üan yüan-liu tsai t'an-t'ao" 太極拳源流再探討 (A further
examination of the origins of t'ai-chi ch'üan). In *Chung-kuo wu-shu shih-liao
chi-k'an*, Vol. 5 (1980): 40–64

Chang Wei-chung 張唯中. "Kuo-shu t'ai-chi ch'üan shih-liao" (Historical materials
on t'ai-chi ch'üan). In *Chung-kuo wu-shu shih-liao chi-k'an*, Vol. 4 (1979): 72–105.

Chang Wei-i 張維一. "Shih-hsi ju-chia ssu-hsiang tui ch'uan-t'ung t'i-yü fa-
chan te ying-hsiang" 試析儒家思想對傳統體育發展的影響 (An
analysis of the influence of Confucian thought on the development of physical
education). *T'i-yü wen-shih*, 1 (1988): 39–43.

Ch'ang Nai-chou 萇乃周. *Ch'ang-shih wu-chi shu* 萇氏武技書 (Ch'ang Nai-
chou's writings on martial arts). Hsü Chen, ed.; Taiwan reprint, n.p., n.d.;
Hsü Chen Preface, 1932; originally published, 1936.

Ch'en Cheng 陳正. "T'ai-chi ch'üan li-lun chung te 'shuang-chung'" 太極拳
理論中的雙重 ("Double-weightedness" in t'ai-chi ch'üan theory). *Wu-
shu chien-shen*, 2 (1986): 34.

Ch'en Ch'ung-jen 陳崇仁. "Chung-kuo ku-tai t'i-yü shih te k'ao-ch'a" 中國
古代體育史的考察 (A study of the history of physical education in
China). In *T'ai-chi ch'üan yen-chiu chuan-chi*, 40, 41, 42, 43, 44, 45 (1970).

Ch'en Hsin 陳鑫. *Ch'en-shih t'ai-chi ch'üan t'u-shuo* 陳氏太極拳圖說 (Ch'en
style t'ai-chi ch'üan). Author's Preface, 1919; first published 1933; reprint
Hong Kong: Ch'en Hsiang-chi shu-chü, 1983.

Ch'en P'an-ling 陳泮嶺. "Ch'ang-chia ch'üan chih yüan-liu k'ao" 萇家拳之
源流考 (A study of the origins of Ch'ang family boxing). *Kuo-shu chou-k'an*.
Photocopy of article in author's collection; year and issue unrecorded; c. 1934,
pp. 32–35.

Ch'en Pin 陳斌. "T'ai-chi ch'üan yü tao-chiao kuan-hsi pien" 太極拳與道教
關係辯 (A discussion of the relationship between t'ai-chi ch'üan and Taoism). *Chung-hua wu-shu*, 5 (1989): 26–27.

Ch'en Shao-tung 陳紹棟. "Lun kuan-yü t'ai-chi ch'üan yüan-liu te i-ke hsin
shuo-fa" 論關於太極拳源流的一個新説法 (A critique of a new
theory on the origins of t'ai-chi ch'üan). *Wu-lin*, 12 (1992): 4–7; also *Ch'i-
kung yü t'i-yü*, 5 (1992): 17–19.

Cheng Chen-k'un 鄭振坤. "Lun Huang Tsung-hsi tui Chung-hua wu-shu te li-

shih kung-hsien" 論黃宗義對中華武術的歷史貢獻 (On Huang
Tsung-hsi's historical contribution to Chinese martial arts). *T'i-yü wen-shih*, 6
(1988): 46–48.

Cheng Chih-lin 鄭志林. "*Chen-chi* yü t'i-yü" 陣紀與體育 (The *Chen-chi* and
physical education). *T'i-yü wen-shih*, 5 (1988): 19–22.

Cheng Man-ch'ing 鄭曼青. *Cheng tzu t'ai-chi ch'üan shih-san p'ien* 鄭子太極拳
十三篇 (Master Cheng's thirteen chapters on t'ai-chi ch'üan). Taipei: Shih-
chung ch'üan-she, 1950.

———. *Cheng tzu t'ai-chi ch'üan tzu-hsiu hsin-fa* 鄭子太極拳自修新法 (Master
Cheng's new method for self-study in t'ai-chi ch'üan). Hongkong: Hsin-lien
ch'u-pan-she, n.d.

Ch'eng Hsiao 程嘯. "Wan-ch'ing Chih-Lu mei-hua ch'üan-hui ch'ien-hsi" 晚
清直魯梅花拳淺析 (An analysis of the late Ch'ing Plum Blossom Boxing
Society in Hebei and Shandong). *Ch'ing-shih yen-chiu t'ung-hsün*, 1 (1988):
26–29.

Ch'eng Ta-li 程大力. "Wu-te jen-hsüeh chung-hsin lun" 武德仁學中心論
(Benevolence at the heart of martial arts ethics). *T'i-yü wen-shih*, 3 (1990):
56–58.

Ch'i Chi-kuang 戚繼光. *Chi hsiao hsin shu* 紀效新書 (New and effective
methods in military science). Ma Ming-ta, ed. Beijing: Jen-men t'i-yü ch'u-
pan-she, 1986.

———. *Lien-ping shih-chi* 練兵實紀 (Practical experience in troop training).
Shang-hai ku-chi ch'u-pan-she, ed., *Ssu-ku ping-chia lei ts'ung-shu*, 1990.

Ch'i Chiang-t'ao 戚江濤. "T'ai-chi ch'üan yüan-liu kuan-kui" 太極拳源流
觀窺 (One view of t'ai-chi ch'üan's origins). *T'ai-chi ch'üan yen-chiu chuan-chi*,
6, 7 (1967).

Chia Chao-shan 賈肇山. "Chia Yao-t'ing yü Wen-wu hsüeh-t'ang" 賈耀亭
與文武學堂 (Chia Yao-t'ing and the Wen-wu Academy). *Wu-lin*, 3 (1989):
6–7.

Chiang Fan 江藩. "Huang Tsung-hsi chuan" 黃宗義傳 (Biography of Huang
Tsung-hsi). *Huang Tsung-hsi ch'üan-chi*, Vol. 12: 74–87.

Chiang Hsin 江新. "Shih-chieh ti-i ping-shu yü san-ta" 世界第一兵書與
散打 (The world's number one book of military strategy and martial arts
sparring). *Chung-hua wu-shu*, 6 (1988): 42–43.

Chiang Jung-ch'iao 姜容樵. "Kuo-shu yüan-liu" 國術源流 (The origins of
Chinese martial arts). *Kuo-shu chou-k'an*, 79–115 (1932–34).

Chiang Wei-chiao 蔣維喬. *Wu-i ch'üan-shu* 武藝全書 (Complete book of
martial arts). Taiwan reprint: Hua-lien ch'u-pan-she, 1983; original n.p.,
n.d.; c. early Republican.

Chiao Lu-pin 焦陸賓. "Chieh-lu p'i-pan wu-shu huo-tung chung te wai-feng hsieh-ch'i" 揭露批判武術活動中的歪風邪氣 (Expose negative tendencies in the martial arts movement). *Hsin t'i-yü*, 3 (1965): 25–27.

Ch'ien T'i-ming 錢惕明. "Yin-fu ching yü wu-shu" 陰符經與武術 (The *Yin-fu ching* and the martial arts). *Wu-lin*, 8 (1990): 12–13.

Chin I-ming 金一明. "Kuo-shu shih-liao nei-jung lüeh-shu" 國術史料內容略述 (An introduction to the content of historical documents on Chinese martial arts). *Kuo-shu chou-k'an*, 103 (1933): 4–6; 104 (1933): 3–4.

———. "Kuo-shu ying i ju-chia wei cheng-tsung" 國術應以儒家為正宗 (Confucianism should be the true philosophy of the martial arts). *Kuo-shu chou-k'an*, 156–57 (1936).

Chin Ting 金鼎. "Wu-lin chiu-shih: hui-ku k'ang-jih chan-cheng ch'ien Che-chiang sheng min-chien wu-shu yün-tung tien-ti" 武林舊事回顧抗日戰爭前浙江省民間武術運動點滴 (Some anecdotes from the world of martial arts: looking back on the Zhejiang popular martial arts movement before the War of Resistance). *T'i-yü shih-liao*, Vol. 10 (1984): 48–53.

Ching Pai 京白. "T'ai-chi ch'üan huo-tung chung te tsao-po pi-hsü ch'ing-ch'u" 太極拳活動中的糟粕必須清除 (We must eliminate negative features in the t'ai-chi ch'üan movement). *Hsin t'i-yü*, 4 (1965): 22–23.

Chou Chien-nan 周建南. "T'ai-chi ch'üan li-shih te yen-chiu" 太極拳歷史的研究 (Research in the history of t'ai-chi ch'üan). In *Chung-kuo wu-shu shih-liao chi-k'an* (1976): 77–99.

Chou Chih-chün 周志俊. "Ch'en Tu-hsiu ch'ien-ch'i t'i-yü ssu-hsiang t'an-t'ao" 陳獨秀前期體育思想探討 (An exploration of Ch'en Tu-hsiu's early thinking on physical education). *T'i-yü wen-shih*, 4 (1988) : 8–11.

Chou Hsi-kuan 周西寬. "Sun Chung-shan yü t'i-yü" 孫中山與體育 (Sun Yat-sen and physical education). *Hsin t'i-yü*, 10 (1981): 25–26.

Chou Lin-I 周林儀. "Lao tzu ssu-hsiang yü t'i-yü pen-chih" 老子思想與體育本質 (Lao tzu's thought and the nature of physical education). *T'i-yü hsüeh-shu yen-t'ao hui chuan-k'an* (1975): 40–48.

Chou Wei-liang 周唯良. "Tui chien-kuo hou wu-shu she-hui k'o-hsüeh li-lun yen-chiu te ssu-k'ao" 對建國後武術社會科學理論研究的思考 (An examination of social science research on the martial arts since the founding of the People's Republic). *Wu-hun*, 4 (1991): 7–8.

Chu Chung-yu 朱仲玉. "Ch'i Chi-kuang ch'iang-shen pao-kuo" 戚繼光強身保國 (Ch'i Chi-kuang strengthened his body and defended the nation). *Hsin t'i-yü*, 1 (1963): 36.

———. "Wen-wu ping-chung te Ku Yen-wu" 文武並重的顧炎武 (Ku Yen-wu's equal emphasis on intellectual and martial development). *Hsin t'i-yü*, 11 (1963): 19–20.

———. "Cheng Ch'eng-kung lien-wu" 鄭成功練武 (Cheng Ch'eng-kung's practice of the martial arts). *Hsin t'i-yü*, 4 (1967): 16.

Chu Te-pao 朱德保. "Chia-ch'iang wu-shu te cheng-li yen-chiu" 加強武術的整理研究 (Improve martial arts research). *Hsin t'i-yü*, 11 (1956): 31.

Ch'üan Tsu-wang 全祖望 "Li-chou hsien-sheng shen-tao pei-wen" 梨州先生神道碑文 (Biography of Huang Tsung-hsi). In *Huang Tsung-hsi ch'üan-chi*, Vol. 12: 1–14.

Chung I 鍾儀. "T'ai-chi ch'üan te li yü yung" 太極拳的理與用 (Theory and applications in t'ai-chi ch'üan). *T'i-yü wen-shih*, 3 (1988): 3.

DeMarco, Michael. "The Origin and Evolution of Taijiquan." *Journal of Asian Martial Arts*, 1 (1992): 9–25.

Donohue, John. *Warrior Dreams: Martial Arts and the American Imagination.* Bergin & Garvey, 1994.

Draeger, Donn. "The Martial-Civil Dicotomy in Asian Combatives" *Hoplos* (Feb. 1981): 6–8.

Feng Fu-ming 馮福明. "T'ai-chi ch'üan yüan-liu k'ao-cheng" 太極拳源流考證 (A study of the origins of t'ai-chi ch'üan). *T'i-yü wen-shih*, 4 (1988): 30–34.

Feng Hsiao-yü 鳳肖玉. "Sui-ch'ao i-ch'ien wu-i yün-tung hsin-li hsüeh ssu-hsiang kuan-k'ui" 隋朝以前武藝運動心理學思想觀窺 (A glimpse of martial arts psychology during the pre-Sui period). *T'i-yü wen-shih*, 1 (1990): 3–5.

Fernandez-Balboa, Juan-Miguel, ed. *Critical Postmodernism in Human Movement, Physical Education, and Sport.* Albany: SUNY Press, 1997.

Fu Chen-lun 傅振倫. "Ts'ung wu-shu te li-shih fa-chan k'an wu-shu te she-hui tso-yung" 從武術的歷史發展看武術的社會作用 (Looking at the social function of the martial arts from the point of view of their historical development). *Ho-nan t'i-yü shih-liao*, 3 (1983): 1–4.

Fu Ch'eng-chiang 傅承江. "Wu-tang ch'üan yü Chung-kuo ku-tai che-hsüeh ssu-hsiang te kuan-hsi" 武當拳與中國古代哲學思想的關係 (The relationship between Wu-tang boxing and ancient Chinese philosophy). *Wu-tang* 1, (1991): 35–38.

Hao Ch'in 郝勤. "Lun li-shih shang t'i-yü yü tsung-chiao te kuan-hsi" 論歷史上體育與宗教的關係 (On the historical relationship between religion and physical education). *T'i-yü wen-shih*, 4 (1988): 12–18.

———. "Lun Chung-kuo wu-shu tui tao-chiao wen-hua te jung-she" 論中國武術對道教文化的融攝 (On the absorption of Taoist culture into the martial arts). *T'i-yü wen-shih*, 1 (1990): 7–11.

Hao Hung-ch'ang 郝鴻昌. "Yüan Nan-ching Chung-yang kuo-shu kuan te kai-k'uang chi tsu-chih chi-kou" 原南京中央國術館的概況及組織

機構 (The general background and organization of the former Nanjing National Martial Arts Academy). *Shao-lin wu-shu*, 5 (1986): 2–8.

Hao Wen 郝文. "*Chou-i yü t'ai-chi ch'üan shu*" 周易與太及拳術 (The *I ching* and t'ai-chi ch'üan). *Wu-lin*, 3 (1987): 4–5.

Henning, Stanley. "The Chinese Martial Arts in Historical Perspective." *Military Affairs*, 45, 4 (1981): 173–78.

———. "Author of Lost Ming Boxing Treatise Identified." *Journal of the Chenstyle Taijiquan Researach Association*, 4, 2 (1996): 63–65.

Ho Liang-ch'en 何良臣. *Chen-chi chu-shih* 陣紀注釋 (*The Science of Warfare* with annotations). Beijing: Chün-shih k'o-hsüeh ch'u-pan-she, 1984.

Hsi Yün-t'ai 習雲太. *Chung-kuo wu-shu shih* 中國武術史 (The history of Chinese martial arts). Beijing: Jen-min t'i-yü ch'u-pan-she, 1985.

Hsiao Chün 蕭軍. "Yu wen-shih che pi yu wu-pei" 有文事者必有武備 (Intellectuals should also practice martial arts). *Hsin t'i-yü*, 12 (1979): 18–20.

Hsiao Pao-yüan 蕭保源. "T'ai-chi ch'üan li ho fa te che-hsüeh chi k'o-hsüeh chih yen-chiu" 太極拳理和法的哲學及科學之研究 (A philosophical and scientific study of the principles and methods of t'ai-chi ch'üan). *T'i-yü hsüeh-shu yen-t'ao hui chuan-k'an* (1975): 266–74.

Hsieh Ming-hsi 謝明習. "Ye t'an t'ai-chi ch'üan fa-chan chung te liu-pi" 也談太及拳發展中的流弊 (A further discussion of negative tendencies in the development of t'ai-chi ch'üan). *Shao-lin wu-shu*, 5 (1988): 20.

Hsin Lan 辛蘭. "Yüeh Fei te wu-i" 岳飛的武藝 (Yüeh Fei's practice of the martial arts). *Hsin t'i-yü*, 2 (1961): 16.

Hsiung Chih-ch'ung 熊志沖. "Man-hua Ming-Ch'ing i-jen te wu-shu piao-yen" 漫話明清藝人的武術表演 (Martial arts street performances during the Ming and Ch'ing dynasties). *Chung-hua wu-shu*, 8 (1985): 38.

———. "Ku-shih chung te wu-shu shih-chieh" 古詩中的武術世界 (Martial arts reflected in ancient poetry). *Wu-shu chien-shen*, 4 (1992): 53–54.

———. "Ch'uan-t'ung t'i-yü yü ch'uan-t'ung wen-hua" 傳統體育與傳統文化 (Traditional physical education and traditional culture). *T'i-yü wen-shih*, 5 (1989): 2–7.

Hsü An-jih 徐安日. "T'ai-chi ch'üan yen-chiu te hsin tung-hsiang" 太極拳研究的新動向 (New directions in t'ai-chi ch'üan research). *Wu-shu chien-shen*, 2 (1991): 2.

Hsü Chen 徐震. *Kuo-chi lun-lüeh* 國技論略 (Summary of the Chinese martial arts). Shanghai: Commercial Press, 1930.

———. *T'ai-chi ch'üan fa-wei* 太極拳發微. (The secrets of t'ai-chi ch'üan). Taipei: Chung-hua wu-shu ch'u-pan-she, 1973; handwritten ms. dated 1941.

———. *T'ai-chi ch'üan k'ao-hsin lu* 太極拳考信錄. (A study of the truth of t'ai-

chi ch'üan). Taipei: Chen-shan-mei ch'u-pan-she, 1965; author preface dated
1936.

———. "Lüeh-lun wu-shu te hsing-chih" 略論武術的性質 (A brief discussion
on the nature of the martial arts). *Hsin t'i-yü*, 3 (1957): 32–34.

Hsü Chi 徐紀. "Yeh-t'an Chung-yang kuo-shu kuan chi ch'i-t'a" 也談中央國
術館及其它 (A discussion of the Central Martial Arts Institute and related
matters). *Chung-hua wu-shu*, 11 (1989): 29–31.

Hsü Lung-hou 許龗厚. *T'ai-chi ch'üan shih t'u-chieh* 太極拳勢圖解 (Illustrated manual of t'ai-chi ch'üan). Taipei: Hua-lien ch'u-pan-she, 1982;
photoreprint of 1921 edition.

Hu Kuang 胡光. "Tui t'ai-chi ch'üan fa-chan chung 'liu-pi' te shang-ch'üeh" 對
太極拳發展中流弊的商榷 (A discussion of "negative tendencies" in
the development of t'ai-chi ch'üan). *Shao-lin wu-shu*, 2 (1988): 32.

———. "Tsai-t'an t'ai-chi ch'üan fa-chan chung te liu-pi" 再談太極拳發展
中的流弊 (A further discussion of errors in the development of t'ai-chi
ch'üan). *Shao-lin yü t'ai-chi*, 6 (1989): 45.

Huang Chao-han 黃兆漢. *Ming-tai tao-shih Chang San-feng k'ao* 明代道士張
三丰考 (A study of the Ming dynasty Taoist Chang San-feng). Taipei:
Hsüeh-sheng shu-chü, 1989.

———. *Tao-chiao yen-chiu lun-wen chi*. 道教研究論文集 (Studies on Taoism).
Hongkong: Chung-wen ta-hsüeh ch'u-pan-she, 1988.

Huang Chien-heng 黃鑑衡. "Sun Chung-shan yü wu-shu" 孫中山與體育
(Sun Chung-shan and the martial arts). *Wu-lin*, 1 (1982): 15.

Huang I 黃易. "Chung-kuo tso-hsieh chu-hsi Pa Chin shuo 'Wen-jen yao hsi-
wu'" 中國作協主席巴金説文人要習武 (Pa Chin, Chairman of the
All-China Writers Association, says: "Literary workers should practice martial
arts"). *Chung-hua wu-shu*, 11 (1987): 37.

Huang Pai-chia 黃百家. "Nei-chia ch'üan-fa"內家拳法 (Art of the Internal
School). In *Chao-tai ts'ung-shu*, Vol. 163.

Huang Ping-hou 黃炳垕. "Huang Li-chou hsien-sheng nien-p'u" 黃梨州先
生年譜 (Chronological biography of Huang Tsung-hsi). In *Huang Tsung-hsi
ch'üan-chi*, Vol. 12: 18–35.

Huang Tsung-hsi 黃宗羲. *Nan-lei chi* 南雷集 (Collected works of Huang
Tsung-hsi). Shanghai: n.p., n.d; photoreprint of 1680 ed.

———. *Huang Tsung-hsi ch'üan-chi* 黃宗羲全集 (Collected works of Huang
Tsung-hsi). Shen Shan-hung, ed. Hangzhou: Che-chiang ku-chi ch'u-pan-
she, 1994.

Huang Wen-chih 黃文志. "Ching-wu t'i-yü hui te nei-wai fa-chan" 精武體
育會的內外發展 (The internal and external development of the Ching-
wu Physical Education Association). *T'i-yü wen-shih*, 1 (1983): 35, 49.

Huang Wen-shan. *Fundamentals of T'ai Chi Chuan*. Hongkong: South Sky Book Company, 1974.

Hung Tun-keng 洪敦耕. "Ch'ien Chung-yang kuo-shu kuan chang-ku" 前中央國術館掌故 (Anecdotes concerning the former National Martial Arts Institute). *Wu-lin*, 99 (1989): 19.

K'ang Ke-wu 康戈武. "T'an-suo ch'üan-chung yüan-liu te fang-fa" 探索拳種源流的方法 (Methods in tracing the origins of martial arts styles). *Chung-hua wu-shu*, 1 (1983): 43–44.

Ku Liu-hsin 顧留馨 and T'ang Hao 唐豪. *T'ai-chi ch'üan yen-chiu* 太極拳研究 (Studies on t'ai-chi ch'üan). Shanghai: 1963.

———. *T'ai-chi ch'üan shu* 太極拳術 (The art of t'ai-chi ch'üan). Shanghai: Shang-hai chiao-yü ch'u-pan-she, 1982.

Ku Po 古柏. "Tui chung-kuo wu-shu ti-wei te wen-hua fan-ssu" 對中國武術地位的文化反思 (A reflection on the role of the martial arts in Chinese culture). *Wu-hun*, 3 (1989): 3.

Ku Tu-tzu 古都子. "Lun nei-chia ch'üan" 論內家拳. (On the Internal School). *Wu-tang*, 2 (1988): 41.

Ku Yüan-kuang 顧元光. "Kuo-shu t'an-yüan" 國術探原 (An investigation into the origins of the martial arts). *Kuo-shu chou-k'an*, 113 (1934): 3.

K'uang Wen-nan 鄺文南. "*Sun tzu ping-fa* yü wu-shu chi-chi ssu-hsiang" 孫子兵法與武術技擊思想 (*Sun tzu's Art of War* and the principles of martial arts). *T'i-yü wen-shih*, 5, (1990): 47–51.

———. "Ping-chia yü wu-shu te t'ung-yüan yü chiao-liu" 兵家與武術的同原與交流 (Military strategy and the martial arts: common origins and exchanges). *T'i-yü wen-shih*, 2 (1990): 27–31.

———. "Chung-hua wu-shu che-hsüeh ssu-hsiang t'an-yüan" 中華武術哲學思想探源 (Tracing the philosophical thought in the martial arts). *Chung-hua wu-shu*, 10 (1988): 18–19.

Kung K'o 龔克. "Wang Tsung-yüeh shih 't'ai-chi ch'üan p'u' te tso-che ma?" 王宗岳是太極拳譜的作者嗎 (Is Wang Tsung-yüeh actually the author of the t'ai-chi classics?). *Chung-hua wu-shu*, 12 (1992): 14.

Kuo Fu-hou 郭福厚. "Nei-chia ch'üan-fa ch'ien-i" 內家拳法淺議 (Brief summary of the *Art of the Internal School*). *Wu-lin*, 7 (1987): 8–9.

Kuo Hsi-fen 郭希汾. *Chung-kuo t'i-yü shih* 中國體育史 (A history of physical education in China). Taipei: Commercial Press, 1967; originally published 1919.

Lei Hsiao-t'ien 雷嘯天. *Chung-kuo wu-shu hsüeh kai-yao* 中國武術學概要 (Summary of the Chinese martial arts). Taipei: Tzu-yu ch'u-pan-she, 1963.

Li Ch'eng 李誠. "Ch'ang Nai-chou Ch'en-kou chieh chih-yu" 萇乃周陳溝結摯友 (Ch'ang Nai-chou makes a close friend in Ch'en Village). *Chung-hua wu-shu*, 11 (1986): 26–27.

Li Chi-fang 李季芳. "Huo Yüan-chia yü Ching-wu t'i-tsao hsüeh-t'ang" 霍元甲與精武體操學堂 (Huo Yüan-chia and the Ching-wu Gymnastics Academy). T'i-yü wen-shih, 5 (1989): 33–35.

Li Chin-chung 黎錦忠. "Tao-chiao ssu-hsiang tui t'ai-chi ch'üan te ying-hsiang" 道教思想對太極拳的影響 (The influence of Taoism on t'ai-chi ch'üan). Chung-hua wu-shu, 1 (1989): 32–33.

Li Ning 李寧. "Hu Shih te t'i-yü kuan" 胡適的體育觀 (Hu Shih's concept of physical education). T'i-yü wen-shih, 3 (1988): 53–55.

Li Pei-hsien 李佩賢. "Ching-wu t'i-yü hui chien-shih" 精武體育會簡史 (A short history of the Ching-wu Physical Education Association). T'i-yü wen-shih, 1 (1983): 34.

Li Yü-ch'iu 李聿求. "Huang Tsung-hsi chuan" 黃宗義傳 (Biography of Huang Tsung-hsi). Huang Tsung-hsi ch'üan-chi, Vol. 12: 88–93.

Liang Ch'i-ch'ao 梁啓超. Chung-kuo chih wu-shih tao 中國之武士道 (Chinese bushido). In Yin-ping-shih ts'ung-shu, Vol. 7. Shanghai: Commercial Press, 1916.

Lin Po-yüan 林伯原. "Wai-chia ch'üan yü nei-chia ch'üan" 外家拳與內家拳 (The External and Internal Schools of the martial arts). Wu-shu chien-shen, 1 (1984): 39–40.

Ling Yüeh-hua 凌躍華. "Ch'ing-tai chiang-nan wu-chü yü Fu-yang wu-hsüeh" 清代江南武舉與富陽武學 (The Ch'ing period military examination system in South China and military studies in Fuyang). Wu-hun, 4 (1985): 25–26.

Liu Ch'ang-lin 劉長林. "Chung-kuo ku-tai yin-yang shuo" 中國古代陰陽說 (The ancient Chinese theory of yin and yang). Wu-hun, 4 (1987): 20–21.

Liu Chün-hsiang 劉峻驤. "Ku-tai che-li yü lun-li tui Chung-kuo wu-shu hsing-ch'eng ho fa-chan te ying-hsiang" 古代哲理與倫理對中國武術形成和發展的影響 (The influence of ancient philosophy and ethics on the formation and development of Chinese martial arts). T'i-yü wen-shih, 5 (1988): 61–66.

Liu Hui-chih 劉會峙, et al. "T'ai-chi ch'üan yüan-liu hsin-t'an" 太極拳源流新探 (A reexamination of the origins of t'ai-chi ch'üan). Wu-tang, 3 (1992): 30–33.

Liu Ping-kuo 劉秉果. "Sung-tai te hsiang-p'u" 宋代的相扑 (Martial arts during the Sung dynasty). T'i-yü shih-liao, Vol. 6 (1982): 37–38.

Lo Tso-yün 羅佐雲. "Tui Yü Ta-yu te Chien-ching tsai-t'an" 對俞大猷劍經再探 (A reexamination of Yü Ta-yu's Classic of Swordsmanship). Wu-lin, 88 (1989): 6–7.

Lu Chao-ming 陸兆明. "Wu-shu chung te yin-yang wu-hsing shuo" 武術中的陰陽五行說 (The yin-yang and five phases theories in the martial arts). T'i-yü wen-shih, 4 (1987): 5–6.

Lu Ch'ung-shan 盧崇善. "Lun 'ye meng Yüan-ti shou-i ch'üan-fa'" 論夜夢元帝授以拳法 (A discussion of the phrase, "At night he [Chang San-feng] dreamt that the God of War taught him the martial arts"). *T'ai-chi ch'üan yen-chiu chuan-chi*, 29 (1969): 28–29.

Lu Ta-chieh 陸達節. *Li-tai ping-shu mu-lu* 歷代兵書目錄. (Catalogue of works on military affairs for each dynasty). Taipei: n.p., 1969; originally published Shanghai, n.p., 1932.

Ma Hung 馬虹. "T'ai-chi t'ai-chi t'u t'ai-chi ch'üan" 太極太極圖太極拳 (T'ai-chi, the t'ai-chi symbol, and t'ai-chi ch'üan). *Wu-lin*, 2 (1991): 22–23.

Ma Ming-ta 馬明達. "Ch'i Chi-kuang *Ch'üan ching* tuan-lun" 戚繼光拳經斷論 (Problems of punctuation in Ch'i Chi-kuang's *Ch'üan-ching*). *Chung-hua wu-shu*, 4 (1985): 32–35; 5 (1985): 25–26.

———. "Ch'ing-tai te wu-chü chih-tu" 清代的武舉制度 (The military examination system during the Ch'ing dynasty). *Chung-hua wu-shu*, 5 (1986): 18–19.

Ma Yüan-nien 馬原年. "Shih-hsi shuang-chung" 試析雙重 (An analysis of "double-weightedness"). *Wu-shu chien-shen*, 3 (1991): 10–11.

Mao Yüan-i 茅元儀. *Wu-pei chih* 武備志. Beijing: Chieh-fang chu-pan-she, 1989.

Matsuda Ryuchi 松田隆智. *Chung-kuo wu-shu-shih-lueh* 中國武術史略 (A brief history of Chinese martial arts). Chongqing: Ssu-ch'uan k'o-hsüeh chi-shu ch'u-pan-she, 1984.

Meng Nai-ch'ang 孟乃昌. "Ch'i Chi-kuang yü t'ai-chi ch'üan" 戚繼光與太極拳 (Ch'i Chi-kuang and t'ai-chi ch'üan). *T'i-yü wen-shih*, 3 (1987): 33–44.

———. "T'ai-chi ch'üan te che-hsüeh chi-ch'u" 太極拳的哲學基礎 (The philosophical foundations of t'ai-chi ch'üan). *T'i-yü wen-shih*, 4 (1987): 47–52.

———. "Lao tzu yü t'ai-chi ch'üan" 老子與太極拳 (Lao tzu and t'ai-chi ch'üan). *Wu-tang*, 1 (1990): 28–33.

Mo Ya 陌雅. "Shang-hai Chung-hua wu-shu hui" 上海中華武術會 (The Shanghai Martial Arts Society). *T'i-yü wen-shih*, 6 (1987): 51.

Mou Chung-chien 牟鍾鑑. "Chung-kuo yüan-shih tsung-chiao yü wu-shu meng-ya" 中國原始宗教與武術萌芽 (China's prehistoric religion and the birth of martial arts). *T'i-yü wen-shih*, 5 (1989): 34–35.

Niu Chia 牛佳. "T'ai-chi ch'üan yü wei-jen chih tao" 太極拳與為人之道 (T'ai-chi ch'üan and ethics). *Chung-hua wu-shu*, 5 (1987): 43.

Pai Yün-feng 白雲峰. "Tui nei-chia ch'üan wu-tzu chüeh te li-chieh" 對內家拳五字訣的理解 (Understanding the five character transmission of the Internal School). *Wu-tang*, 2 (1988): 11; *Shao-lin wu-shu*, 4 (1987): 14.

———. "Shih-lun t'ai-chi ch'üan fa-chan chung te liu-pi" 試論太極拳發展中的流弊 (A preliminary discussion of negative tendencies in the development of t'ai-chi ch'üan). *Shao-lin wu-shu*, 2 (1987): 28–29.

Parsons, James. *The Peasant Rebellions of the Late Ming Dynasty*. Ann Arbor, Michigan: Association for Asian Studies, 1970.

Pien Jen-chieh 卞人杰. *Kuo-chi kai-lun* 國技概論 (Outline of the Chinese martial arts). Taipei: Chen-shan-mei ch'u-pan-she, 1971; Taipei: Hua-lien ch'u-pan-she, 1972; originally published 1936.

Po Ch'i 伯奇. "Sung-tai te wu-hsüeh" 宋代的武學 (Martial studies during the Sung dynasty). *Chung-kuo wu-shu*, 2 (1987): 6.

———. "Ch'ing-tai huang-ti te wu-kung" 清代皇帝的武功 (The Ch'ing dynasty emperor's practice of the martial arts). *Chung-hua wu-shu*, 4 (1985): 15.

Price, Maurice T. "Differentiating Myth, Legend, and History in Ancient Chinese Culture." *American Anthropologist*, XLVIII, 1946: 31–42.

Seidel, Anna. "A Taoist Immortal of the Ming Dynasty: Chang San-feng." In Wm. Theodore de Bary, ed. *Self and Society in Ming Thought*. New York: Columbia University Press, 1970.

Shang-hai ku-chi ch'u-pan-she 上海古籍出版社, ed. *Ssu-k'u ping-chia lei ts'ung-shu* 四庫兵家類叢書 (Military writings from the *Ssu-k'u Collection*). Shanghai: Shang-hai ku-chi ch'u-pan-she, 1990.

Shao Chüan 邵雋. "Ching-wu t'i-yü hui te fa-chan chi ch'i ying-hsiang" 精武體育會的發展及其影響 (The development and influence of the Ching-wu Physical Eduation Association). *T'i-yü wen-shih*, 1 (1990): 16–20.

Shao T'ing-ts'ai 邵廷采. "I-hsien Huang Wen-hsiao hsien-sheng chuan" 遺獻黃孝文先生傳 (Biography of Huang Tsung-hsi). *Huang Tsung-hsi ch'üan-chi*, Vol. 12: 61–67.

Shen Shou 沈壽. "T'ai-chi ch'üan fa yen-chiu" 太極拳法研究 (Studies on t'ai-chi ch'üan). Fuzhou: Fu-chien jen-min ch'u-pan-she, 1984.

Sheng Ch'ing 聖慶. "Tsai fu-ku chung ch'iu-te chieh-tuo" 在復古中求得解脫 (In search of an escape from the revivalist movement). *Wu-hun*, 3 (1989): 13.

Struve, Lynn A. *The Ming-Qing Conflict, 1619–1683: A Historiography and Source Guide*. Ann Arbor, Michigan: Association for Asian Studies, 1998.

Su Ching-ts'un 蘇競存. "Wu-shu yü nung-min ko-ming" 武術與農民革命 (Martial arts and peasant revolutions). *T'i-yü wen-shih*, 3 (1990): 42–43.

———. "San-shih nien-tai te t'i-yü chün-shih-hua ssu-hsiang" 三十年代的體育軍事化思想 (The militarization of physical education during the 1930s). *Hsin t'i-yü*, 4 (1987): 18–21.

———. "Hsin-hai ko-ming ch'ien-hou te chün-kuo-min chiao-yü te t'i-yü ssu-hsiang" 辛亥革命前後的軍國民教育的體育思想 (Physical education in the national military education program during the late Ch'ing-early Republican period). *T'i-yü wen-shih*, 1 (1988):19–22.

———. "Liang Ch'i-ch'ao te shang-wu ssu-hsiang yü min-tsu t'i-yü te hsing-chüeh" 梁啓超的尚武思想與民族體育的醒覺 (Liang Ch'i-ch'ao's military thinking and the development of national physical education aware-ness). *T'i-yü wen-shih*, 3 (1989): 22–25.

Su Hsiao-ch'ing 蘇肖晴. "K'ang Yu-wei te t'i-yü ssu-hsiang chi ch'i ch'eng-yin" 康有為的體育思想及其成因 (K'ang Yu-wei's views on physical edu-cation). *T'i-yü wen-shih*, 1 (1988): 49–52.

Su Hsiung-fei 蘇雄飛. "K'ung tzu te t'i-yü k'o-ch'eng lun, fang-fa lun, chi ch'i p'ing-chia" 孔子的體育課程論方法論及其評價 (The role of physical education in Confucius' curriculum, its methodology, and an evaluation), *T'i-yü hsüeh-shu yen-t'ao hui chuan-k'an*, 1975: 33–39.

Su T'ung-feng 蘇桐鳳. "T'ai-chi ch'üan yüan-liu shu-yao" 太極拳源流述要 (Sketch of the origins of t'ai-chi ch'üan). In *Chung-kuo wu-shu shih-liao chi-k'an*, Vol. 2, 1976.

Sun Kuo-chung 孫國中. "Chi-hsiao hsin-shu, 'Ch'üan-ching chieh-yao p'ien' pu-hsü" 紀效新書拳經捷要篇補續 (Supplementary notes to the *Classic of Pugilism*). *T'i-yü wen-shih*, 1 (1988): 25.

Sun Lu-t'ang 孫祿堂. *T'ai-chi ch'üan hsüeh* 太極拳學 (The study of t'ai-chi ch'üan). Hongkong: Hsiang-kang wu-shu ch'u-pan-she, n.d.; preface dated 1919.

Sun Pao-yin 孫豹隱. "Yen Hsi-chai yü wen-wu chih tao" 顏習齋與文武之道 (Yen Yüan and the way of combining the civil and the martial). *Wu-lin*, 119 (1991): 17–18.

———. "Wen-wu ch'üeh-i ch'i tao hu?" 文武缺一豈道乎 (If the intellectual and martial are not combined, the tao is not complete). *Wu-shu chien-shen*, 1 (1994): 49.

Sun Wen 孫文 (Chung-shan 中山). "Ching-wu pen-chi hsü" 精武本紀序 (Inscription on the occasion of the tenth anniversay of the Ching-wu Physical Education Association). Reprinted in *T'i-yü wen-shih*, 1 (1983): 35.

Sutton, Nigel. "Gongfu, Guoshu, and Wushu: State Appropriation of the Martial Arts in Modern China." *Journal of Asian Martial Arts*, 3 (1993): 102–14.

Tanaka, Steven. "Imaging History: Inscribing Belief in the Nation." *Journal of Asian Studies*, 1 (1994): 24–44.

T'an Pen-lun 譚本倫. "Lun Wu-tang Sung-hsi p'ai nei-chia ch'üan" 論武當松溪派內家拳 (On the Wu-tang Sung-hsi p'ai lineage of the Internal School). *Wu-tang*, 1 (1991): 15.

T'ang Hao 唐豪. "Chiu Chung-kuo t'i-yü shih shang fu-hui te Ta-mo" 舊中國體育史上附會的達摩 (Falsifications concerning the role of Bodhidharma in the history of Chinese physical education). In *Chung-kuo t'i-yü shih ts'an-k'ao tzu-liao*, Vol. 4, 1958.

———. *Nei-chia ch'üan te yen-chiu* 內家拳的研究 (A study of the Internal School). Hongkong: Unicorn Press, 1969; originally published 1935.

————. *Wang Tsung-yüeh t'ai-chi ch'üan ching yen-chiu* 王宗岳太極拳經研究 (A study of Wang Tsung-yüeh's t'ai-chi ch'üan classics). Hongkong: Unicorn Press, 1969; originally published 1935.

————. *T'ai-chi ch'üan te ken-yüan* 太極拳的根源 (The roots of t'ai-chi ch'üan). Hongkong: Hsiang-kang ch'üan-shu yen-chiu-she, n.d.; originally published 1935.

————. "T'ai-chi ch'üan te yüan-yüan yü liu-yen" 太極拳的淵源與流演 (The origins and development of t'ai-chi ch'üan). In *Chung-kuo wu-shu shih-liao chi-k'an*, Vol. 2, 1976.

————. "Ch'ing-tai ya-p'o hsia te wu-shih chi ch'i chu-tso" 清代壓迫下的武士及其著作 (Martial artists and their writings during the period of Manchu repression). *Kuo-shu chou-k'an*, 161–69, 1936.

————. *Hsing-chien chai sui-pi* 行健齋隨筆 (Miscellaneous writings from the Hsing-chien studio). Shanghai: Shanghai-shih kuo-shu kuan, 1937.

————. *Shen-chou wu-i* 神洲武藝 (China's martial arts). Kirin: Chi-lin wen-shih ch'u-pan-she, 1986.

Teng Shih-hai 鄧時海, ed. *T'ai-chi ch'üan k'ao* 太極拳考 (Studies on t'ai-chi ch'üan). Hongkong: Tung-ya t'u-shu kung-ssu, 1980.

T'ien Yung-p'eng 田永鵬. "Ch'uan-t'ung wu-shu yü ku-tai tsung-chiao i-shih ch'ien-t'an" 傳統武術與古代宗教意識淺探 (A preliminary examination of traditional martial arts and ancient religious consciousness). *T'i-yü wen-shih*, 3 (1988): 28–29.

Ts'ang Hsiao-chung 藏孝忠. "Sun tzu ping-fa yü chi-chi" 孫子兵法與技擊 (*Sun tzu's Art of War* and the martial arts). *Wu-lin*, 4 (1988): 8–9.

————. "Wu-shu yen-chiu wen-t'i te t'an-shu" 武術研究問題的探述 (An examination of problems in martial arts research). *T'i-yü wen-shih*, 3 (1988): 6.

Tsao Ping-jen 曹秉仁. *Ning-po fu-chih* 寧波府志 (Ningbo prefectual gazetteer), 1735.

Tseng Chao-jan 曾昭然. *T'ai-chi ch'üan ch'üan-shu* 太極拳全書 (The complete book of t'ai-chi ch'üan). Hongkong: Yu-lien ch'u-pan-she, 1960.

Tseng Ch'ing-tsung 曾慶宗. "T'ai-chi tao-chiao ho shui: t'ai-chi ch'üan che-li t'an-suo" 太極道教和水太極拳哲理探索 (T'ai-chi, Taoism, and water: tracing the philosophical principles of t'ai-chi ch'üan). *Wu-lin*, 4 (1988): 42–43.

Wang Chien 王劍. "Ch'uan-t'ung wu-shu wa-chüeh cheng-li te li yü pi" 傳統武術挖掘整理的利與弊 (Positive and negative tendencies in the rediscovery and revival of the martial arts). *T'i-yü wen-shih*, 3 (1988): 2.

Wang Chih-yung 王致涌. "Wo-kuo tsui tsao te t'i-yü hui" 我國最早的體育會 (China's first physical education association). *Hsin t'i-yü*, 11 (1981): 21–22.

Wang Chuang-fei 王壯飛. "Kuo-shu te yüan-liu" 國術的源流 (The origins of the martial arts). *Kuo-shu chou-k'an*, 89 (1933): 2–3.

Wang Chüeh-hsin 王玨鑫. "Kuo-shu li-shih chih ho-li t'an-ch'iu" 國術歷史之合理探求 (A rational approach to research in martial arts history). *Chung-kuo wu-shu shih-liao chi-k'an*, Vol. 3 (1976): 1–8.

Wang Ch'ung-wu 王崇武. "Ming Ch'eng-tsu yü fang-shih" 明成祖與方士 (Ming dynasty Emperor Ch'eng-tsu and the Taoists). In *Chung-kuo she-hui ching-chi shih chi-k'an*, 8, 1, 1949.

Wang Hao-jan 王浩然 and Ma Ch'ing-hai 馬青海. "Huang Pai-chia *Nei-chia ch'üan-fa* chin-shih" 黃百家內家拳法今釋 (Colloquial translation of Huang Pai-chia's *Art of the Internal School*). *T'i-yü wen-shih*, 6 (1983): 18–21.

Wang Hsi-an 王錫安. "Yin-yang hsüeh-shuo yü Chung-kuo ch'uan-t'ung wu-shu" 陰陽學說與中國傳統武術 (The yin-yang theory and the traditional martial arts). *T'i-yü wen-shih*, 2 (1988): 3, 21.

Wang Huai 王槐. "Tao-chiao yang-sheng-shu yü t'ai-chi ch'üan" 道教養生術與太極拳 (Taoist health practices and t'ai-chi ch'üan). *Wu-tang*, 4 (1992): 23–24, 26.

Wang K'e-chün 王克俊. "Yü Ta-yu hsi-wu wei-min" 俞大猷習武衛民 (Yü Ta-yu practiced marial arts and defended the nation). *Hsin t'i-yü*, 9 (1963): 17–18.

Wang Tzu-hsin 王資鑫. "T'ai-chi ch'üan che-yüan t'an" 太極拳哲源探 (An exploration of the philosophical sources of t'ai-chi ch'üan). *Chung-hua wu-shu*, 2 (1988): 11–13.

Wei Ju-lin 魏汝霖, Liu Chung-p'ing 劉仲平. *Chung-kuo chün-shih ssu-hsiang shih* 中國軍事思想史 (A history of Chinese military thought). Taipei: Li-ming wen-hua shih-yeh ku-fen yu-hsien kung-ssu, 1968.

Wen Chung 聞鍾. "Li-tai ping-shu chung yu nei-hsieh wu-i shu-chi" 歷代兵書中有哪些武藝書籍 (What writings on martial arts can be found in the literature of military science). In *Chung-kuo wu-shu shih-liao chi-k'an*, Vol. 2 (1976): 92–94.

Weng-chou lao-min 翁州老民. "Huang Tsung-hsi chuan" 黃宗義傳 (Biography of Huang Tsung-hsi). *Huang Tsung-hsi ch'üan-chi*, Vol. 12: 68.

Wile, Douglas, trans. *Master Cheng's Thirteen Chapters on T'ai-chi ch'üan*. New City, New York: Sweet Ch'i Press, 1982.

———. trans. *T'ai-chi Touchstones: Yang Family Secret Transmissions*. New City, New York: Sweet Ch'i Press, 1983.

———. trans. *Cheng Man-ch'ing's Advanced T'ai-chi Form Instructions with Selected Writings on Medicine, the I ching, Meditation, and the Arts*. New City, New York: Sweet Ch'i Press, 1985.

————. *Art of the Bedchamber: The Chinese Sexual Yoga Classics, Including Women's Solo Meditation Texts.* Albany: SUNY Press, 1992.

————. *Lost T'ai-chi Classics from the Late Ch'ing Dynasty.* Albany: SUNY Press, 1996.

Wong, James I. *A Source Book in the Chinese Martial Arts.* Stockton, California: Koinonia Publications, 1978.

Wong, Shui-hon. "The Cult of Chang San-feng." *Journal of Oriental Studies* 17 (1979): 10–53.

Wu Chih-ch'ing 吳志青. *Kuo-shu li-lun kai-yao* 國術理論概要 (Summary of Chinese martial arts theory). In *Kuo-min ts'ung-shu.* Taipei: National Library, series 1, Vol. 50, 1989; originally published 1930.

Wu Hsü 吳緒. "Pei-ching t'i-yü yen-chiu-she yü chin-tai Chung-kuo wu-shu te fa-chan" 北京體育研究社與近代中國武術的發展 (The Beijing Physical Education Research Institute and the development of modern Chinese martial arts). *T'i-yü wen-shih,* 6 (1990): 34–37.

Wu T'eng-ta 吳騰達. "Yen Hsi-chai te t'i-yü ssu-hsiang" 顏習齋的體育思想 (Yen Yüan's thought on physical education). *T'i-yü hsüeh-shu yen-t'ao-hui chuan-k'an,* 1975: pp. 280–88.

Wu T'u-nan 吳圖南. *T'ai-chi ch'üan chih yen-chiu* 太極拳之研究 (A study of t'ai-chi ch'üan). Hongkong: Shang-wu yin-shu kuan, 1984.

Wu Wen-chung 吳文忠. *Chung-kuo t'i-yü fa-chan shih* 中國體育發展史 (History of the development of Chinese physical education). Taipei: San-min shu-chü, 1987.

————. "Chung-kuo wu-shu fa-chan chien-shih" 中國武術發展簡史 (A brief history of the development of Chinese martial arts). *Chung-kuo wu-shu shih-liao chi-k'an,* Vol. 2 (1975): 1.

————. *Chung-kuo chin pai nien t'i-yü shih* 中國近百年體育史 (The past one hundred years of Chinese physical education). Taipei: Commercial Press, 1967.

Wu Wen-han 吳文翰. "Ch'ing-tai te wu-ch'ang k'ao-shih" 清代的武場考試 (The practical examination for military service during the Ch'ing period). *Wu-shu chien-shen,* 5 (1990): 51–53.

Yang Ch'eng-fu 楊澄甫. *T'ai-chi ch'üan shih-yung fa* 太極拳使用法 (Self-defense applications of t'ai-chi ch'üan). Taipei: Chung-hua wu-shu ch'u-pan-she, 1974; originally published 1931.

————. *T'ai-chi ch'üan t'i-yung ch'üan-shu* 太極拳體用全書 (Complete principles and practices of t'ai-chi ch'üan). Shanghai: Chung-hua shu-chu, 1948; originally published 1934.

Yang Chih-ts'ai 楊志才. " 'Yeh meng Hsüan-ti shou chih ch'üan-fa' wo-chien" 夜夢玄帝授之拳法我見(My view of the phrase "[Chang San-feng] received a martial art in a dream from the God of War"). *Wu-tang*, 1 (1994): 15–16.

Yang Shao-yü 楊紹虞. "Ch'ang-tuan ta chi ch'i-t'a: tu *Wu-pien* cha-chi." 長短打及其他讀武編札記 (Long and short fighting and other questions: notes on reading the *Wu-pien*). *Chung-hua wu-shu*, 7 (1988): 34–35.

———. "Shen-tao hsüan-hsüeh yü wu-shu yün-tung" 神道玄學與武術運動 (Mysticism, metaphysics, and the martial arts movement). *Wu-tang*, 3 (1990): 21–30.

Yang Ting-hsin 楊丁新. "Wu-ssu yün-tung yü t'i-yü" 五四運動與體育 (The May Fourth Movement and physical education). *Hsin t'i-yü*, 5 (1979): 2–6.

———. "Hsü yü shih" 虛與實 (Empty and full). *Chung-hua wu-shu*, 6 (1988): 46.

Yang Yung 楊永. "Hsien yu nei-chia ch'üan hou yu Chang San-feng" 先有內家拳後有張三丰 (The Internal School predates Chang San-feng). *T'i-yü wen-shih*, 4 (1987): 16.

Yü Chien-hua 于建華. "T'ai-chi ch'üan li-lun te che-hsüeh chi-ch'u ch'u-t'an" 太極拳理論的哲學基礎初探 (A preliminary discussion of the philosophical foundations of t'ai-chi ch'üan theory). *Che-chiang t'i-yü k'o-hsüeh*, 3 (1986): 10–13.

Yü Chih-chün 于志俊. "Wu-tang nei-chia ch'üan te ch'üan-li shih k'o-hsüeh hai-shih hsüan-hsüeh" 武當內家拳的拳理是科學還是玄學 (Is Wu-tang internal boxing theory science or metaphysics?). *Wu-tang*, 6 (1991): 35–37.

Yung Yang-jen 雍陽人. "T'ai-chi ch'üan yüan-liu k'ao-cheng" 太極拳源流考證 (A study of the origins of t'ai-chi ch'üan). *T'i-yü wen-shih*, 4 (1988): 21–27.

Index

CPSIA information can be obtained at www.ICGtesting.com
Printed in the USA
LVOW05s0950130713

342694LV00001B/57/P